Boot Camp for the Married Woman's Soul

Bible Study

Christi Robillard

Stoney Creek Publishers † United States

Published by Stoney Creek Publishers: 15550 Stoney Creek Drive, Riverside, California 92504

ISBN-13: 978-0-615-71078-5 (Stoney Creek Publishers)
ISBN-10: 0615710786

To my Larry—in all my ways and in all my days,
I love you

Contents

Introduction

Welcome to *BOOT CAMP for the Married Woman's Soul*! Change is hard! In order for a person to successfully retrain their thinking and actions it takes diligence and persistence with a purpose in view. Your purpose is to gain *new understanding* about yourself, your husband, and your marriage.

Each lesson is designed to be done over a two week period but can be done in one week increments. This study is best suited for small groups and is not intended to replace traditional Bible studies, but rather it should be considered a companion study.

There are five distinct sections within each lesson. The ***RECAPTURE*** section will focus on biblical basic truths about specific areas of marriage. The ***RECONNECT*** section will focus on aligning your heart with biblical truths about marriage. The ***REDIRECT*** section will help direct your thoughts with what you have just studied in a very practical way.

The ***DAILY HOMEWORK*** section should begin after completion of the first three sections. This is the most important aspect of the lesson; this is where you will put into practice what you are learning! There will also be a ***DIARY*** section at the very end of your Daily Homework, don't skip this last section! The Diary section is where you will evaluate and record new understanding that you have gained through your study. You will even have the opportunity to record positive comments made to you by your husband or others who noticed your progress!

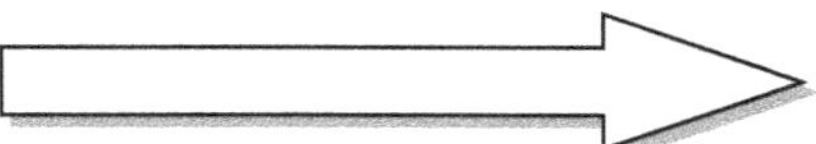

Be encouraged by Daniel 10:12, "…for from the first day that you set your heart on understanding this and on humbling yourself before your God, your words were heard…"

To *set your heart* in the Hebrew literally means to "gain understanding." Let's "gain understanding" about husbands and marriage. Let's agree with this word from Daniel; "*to set your heart on understanding this and humbling yourself before your God,*" that this *BOOT CAMP* will give new insights that will help change you and your marriage!

BOOT CAMP Guidelines

1. You will be challenged! These lessons are hard, that's why this study is called BOOT CAMP!

2. Go through the lessons slowly and methodically. Be careful to *read* each question and *follow the instructions.*

3. Your goal is to have "real" answers – not "right" answers.

4. Some of the questions may seem repetitive or redundant – there is a purpose for this. You will be led through slightly different aspects of each topic in order to gain deeper understanding. Be diligent to dig deep with each question even if it *appears* you may have already answered a similar question.

5. Don't look ahead – stay focused on the lesson that you are working on.

6. You may see immediate results – or you may not. Be prepared for this to take time as you practice what you are learning.

7. This is a study which covers personal and intimate topics. Everything that is shared in this study group stays in this study group. While sharing is encouraged to be candid, please respect your marriage, your husband, and yourself by sharing thoughtfully during group discussion time.

8. This is your time! Each woman should fully participate in the group discussion time. You have something to add; whether it's a comment or a question. If it matters to you it will matter to someone else.

9. There are only eight lessons. Please schedule appointments on other days. Do your best to make each meeting and be on time, the discussion time will go by fast as you will discover!

Mission Statement

BOOT CAMP for the Married Woman's Soul is a biblically based married women's study. There is strong emphasis on truth from the infallible Word of God as the foundation and direction for maintaining the sanctity of marriage within this study. The Word of God is clear and implicit on the topic of marriage; it is held in the highest regard and meant to endure a lifetime.

Several years ago I was asked this question by a woman during a question and answer period following a lecture I had just given, "What do you think is the greatest problem women in the church have?" Immediately a verse came to mind, "...Is it well with your husband? Is it well with the child?" 2 Kings 4:26. My reply began with this verse, it was as if I didn't need to say another word, but I did!

Good marriages don't just happen—disasters just happen! The devil has ramped up his strategies against the Church regarding marriage. How do we know this? Divorce in the church is literally at epidemic levels and primarily among life-long marriages of twenty five years and longer! The Church needs to ramp up their strategies too! The Church needs to be on the offense instead of the defense against this war. *Every* marriage needs protection. *Every* married couple needs to be *proactive* in their marriage. *Every* married couple needs to be actively working on, encouraging, and strengthening their marriage!

Consider this: Polio was a devastating disease that caused nearly 3,000 deaths in the United States alone and thousands more were left with disabilities. It was a feared crippler and often a death sentence to the afflicted. The United States led the war, and it was a war, on polio! In 1955 when the polio vaccine, created by Jonas Salk, became widely available polio was virtually eliminated from the United States by 1979 and the Western hemisphere by 1991!

Approximately 3,000 deaths due to polio alone; an epidemic. Consider the millions of divorces that have occurred within the Church, another epidemic! What if the Church had the same mind and the same dedication towards eliminating divorce? Families would be strengthened; schools, communities, government, and the world! Godly marriages are the backbone of peace and order, and a replica of the Christians relationship to Christ. It's no wonder the devil hates marriage so much! If we don't, who will?

BOOT CAMP for the Married Woman's Soul is one more strategy in the war on divorce. It is my most sincere prayer that God would use this study to straighten out crooked thoughts about marriage, to encourage enjoyment in marriage, and to stimulate life-long marital commitments, as God designed marriage to be.

~ *Christi Robillard*

"Vestigia nulla retrorsum!"
No stepping back!

"Is it well with your husband...?"

2 Kings 4:26

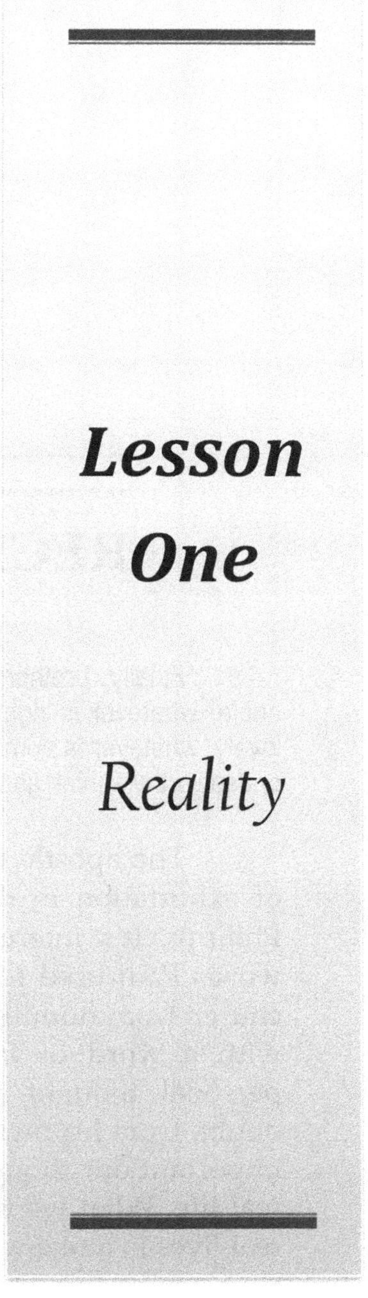

Everyone has a thought life. We think about things that have happened or may happen. We think about what is real and what is not real. We even talk to ourselves. But have you ever considered how your thoughts can affect your *real* life and your relationships? Your thought life has a powerful effect on your everyday life and your relationships, this is why: the Bible says, "For as he thinketh in his heart, so is he..." (Proverbs 23:7 KJV). Your thoughts really do become a part of who you are!

As creatures of habit, we effortlessly jump on our mental treadmill and proceed through the day with thoughts that are based on truth and thoughts that are based on flat out lies! It's so easy to get on the *thought life treadmill!* Beginning with first thoughts in the morning to last thoughts while falling asleep at night; and it is a treadmill! Consider this: when was the last time you had a *new* and *positive* thought concerning your husband or your marriage relationship? If it's been awhile, you are on that treadmill and it's time to get off!

Let's *recapture* truths from Scripture about the importance of your thought life and how important it is to maintain positive and true thoughts about the one you are married to and your marriage relationship in general. This can be a *reality* check!

RECAPTURE

Finally, brothers, whatever is true, whatever is noble, whatever is right, whatever is pure, whatever is lovely, whatever is admirable – if anything is excellent or praiseworthy – think about such things. Philippians 4:8

The apostle Paul is giving a final word of exhortation in this verse to the church in Philippi. It's interesting that after all of the words Paul used to exhort and encourage the church from humility to harmony that he ends with a word of instruction about our own personal thought life! Paul understood, no doubt, from his own personal experience, how important our thought life is in relation to our real life. What we think about will impact our real lives in a real way!

Why so many words, couldn't Paul have used just one really good word to sum it all up? Yes, of course he could have. Let's take a closer look at this verse and see what gain there is by Paul using *eight* different adjectives to describe what we are to think on.

- Using a dictionary, **look up each of these words and record their definitions.**

    - True

    - Noble

    - Right

    - Pure

    - Lovely

    - Admirable

    - Excellent

    - Praiseworthy

Already you have a deepened understanding of the importance for each word selected by Paul in his instruction. The point of this exercise is to *recapture* biblical truth about your thought life, and there is no better way than to take the time to contemplate each word chosen by the inspiration of the Holy Spirit to stimulate a truthful and peaceful thought life.

➢ Now for a different perspective, **read** Jeremiah 29:11 and **record** the verse below, (NASB is best for this verse).

✝ Plans and thoughts are words that are used interchangeably depending on which Bible version you are reading. **Record *three* "thoughts" or "plans" the Lord has regarding you?**

1. ______________________

2. ______________________

3. ______________________

- What does the Lord say are ***not*** His thoughts or plans towards you?

Now record dictionary definitions for:

- Welfare
- Future
- Hope
- Calamity

"…You must bring him to a condition in which he can practice self-examination for an hour without discovering any of those facts about himself which are perfectly clear to anyone who has ever lived in the same house with him or worked with him in the same office."

~ C. S. Lewis

Screwtape Letters

- As a result of your word study from Philippians 4:8 and Jeremiah 29:11, what new appreciation have you gained for the types of thoughts you are to have, in light of the types of thoughts/plans God already has for you?

Isn't it wonderful to know that the thought life of the Most High God towards you is *for welfare, to give you a hope and a future*? Now consider your thought life, and be real—this is a lesson titled "Reality."

What thoughts do you <u>really</u> have towards your: (no phrases please, use as many single words as you can think of).

Husband:

Marriage:

- Did you find yourself in *contrast* to God's thoughts or did you *connect*? **How does this make you feel? (Share in detail your discovery)**

> "All a man's ways seem right to him, but the LORD weighs the heart."
> Proverbs 21:2

RECONNECT

In this next section you will work at aligning your heart with what is true and real according to God's word about your thought life.

Your thought life is the most influential part of your being. It can help make you or it can help break you! What takes place in your mind truly leads to what takes place in the reality of your daily life!
In Hebrews 4:12 we are told, "For the word of God is living and active. Sharper than any

double-edged sword, it penetrates even to dividing soul and spirit, joints and marrow; it *judges the thoughts and attitudes of the heart."*

Sometimes we can literally get lost in our thought life and no longer be an accurate judge of what is real in regard to our thoughts. Have you ever asked yourself, "Am I thinking right about this...?" Of course you have, we all have. No one else knows our private thought life better than God. But this is our hope: we have an all knowing God who is more than willing to help us with our thoughts. We can literally ask God to "judge our thoughts," and He will, and we need that!

- For your next exercise please stop and take some time to ask God with a sincere heart to *judge* your thoughts as you work through this next section—it will make the difference between doing busy work or allowing God to speak to you very personally.

Review Philippians 4:8 as you will work from the words in that verse.

- **Use your dictionary definitions from the last section as a guide:**

Record three ***true*** positive thoughts about your husband.

1.

2.

3.

Record three ***noble*** thoughts about your husband.

1.

2.

3.

Record three ***right*** thoughts about your husband.

1.

2.

3.

Record three ***pure*** thoughts about your husband.

1.

2.

3.

> "The wise in heart accept commands, but a chattering fool comes to ruin."
> Proverbs 10:8

- Very honestly, how much time have you spent this past week thinking (*positive*) *true* thoughts; *noble* thoughts, *right* thoughts, and/or *pure* thoughts about your husband?

Now this next question requires that you look at *the fruit* of your thought life. I don't think we think very often about the fact that our thought life actually produces fruit, but it does. Our thought life can produce good fruit or it can produce rotten fruit!

- Based on how you answered the last question (either, or): what type of fruit has been produced so far by your current thought life, please be specific? How does this make you feel?

- Now you will do the same exercise regarding thoughts about your marriage from the remaining words of Philippians 4:8 **using your dictionary definitions.**

Record three ***lovely*** thoughts about your marriage.

1.

2.

3.

Record three ***admirable*** thoughts about your marriage.

1.

2.

3.

Record three ***excellent*** thoughts about your marriage.

1.

2.

3.

Record three ***praiseworthy*** thoughts about your marriage.

1.

2.

3.

- Ask yourself this question: How well has your current thought life served you thus far? Record your thoughts:

To illustrate the power of a woman's thought life; let's look at a story from 2 Samuel about David's wife Michal, *the daughter of Saul*.

- **Read 2 Samuel 6: 16–23.**

"Wisdom involves knowing God and the subtleties of the human heart. More than knowledge, is the right application of knowledge in moral and spiritual matters, in handling dilemmas, in negotiating complex relationships."
~ J. Oswald Sanders
Spiritual Leadership

- **Fill in the blank spaces with the appropriate words.**

"Have you realized that most of your unhappiness in life is due to the fact that you are listening to yourself instead of talking to yourself?"
~ Martyn Loyd-Jones
Spiritual Depression

1. From verse 16, "…Michal the daughter of Saul…she__________________in her heart."

____

2. From verse 20, "…Michal the daughter of Saul came out to meet him and

____

____

3. From verse 23, "And Michal the daughter of Saul had no

______________________________________."

Did you notice the sad progression throughout these verses? Scripture tells us that Michal *despised* David in her heart. Michal's thoughts turned into words, and her words turned into a real destiny. Although Michal was married to David all her days, she was remembered in these verses as "the daughter of Saul," not David's wife!

If you were to have a cup of coffee with Michal today, no doubt, she would have her list of reasons as to why she despised David. However, Michal's thought life did not serve her well as we read from verse 23, she had "…no children until the day of her death."

Every one of us will have a last day. The question is: will it be a lonely and sad day because of the thoughts you have cultivated in your mind and in your heart?

This is a strong exhortation to ponder. You should seriously evaluate your thought life and play it out to its conclusion seeing where it leads you!

➤ **Read** and **record** each verse in the space given. Give careful heed to the instruction and wisdom contained within:

- Proverbs 4:23

- Proverbs 12:25

- Proverbs 23:7a

- Matthew 12:34b

✝ Which Scripture verse speaks most directly to you today? Record your thoughts:

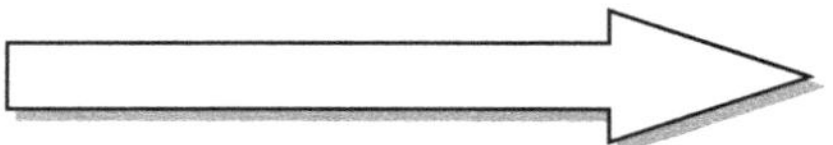

REDIRECT

This section of the lesson will pull together the thoughts and themes from the other two sections by offering practical suggestions with daily homework.

By this point you have made some real discoveries about your own thought life. Maybe you have never really connected the two before; the power of your thought life to what is taking place in your real life.

- Do you now realize that your personal thought life has real power over what takes place in your marriage?

When you indulge your thought life in negative thoughts about your husband and marriage you really do set yourself up for a fall! If you recognize today that your thought life is producing rotten fruit you need to take drastic measures to redirect your thoughts.

- Reflecting on Hebrews 4:12, you learned that God's word is able to literally judge your thoughts. When you are praying daily and spending time in the Word, ask God to *judge your thoughts.*

- Wouldn't it be so much easier if your mind could literally have a harness on it and get jerked every time it disobeyed? The words that Paul used in Philippians 4:8 really can be that "harness" for the mind as you meditate on them.

> Finally, brothers, whatever is ***true***, whatever is ***noble***, whatever is ***right***, whatever is ***pure***, whatever is ***lovely***, whatever is ***admirable*** – if anything is ***excellent*** or ***praiseworthy*** – THINK [dwell], about such things.
>
> Philippians 4:8

Train Your Mind

- Write Philippians 4:8 on a three-by-five card highlighting the adjectives from your word study. Put the card where you will see it frequently; your refrigerator, vanity mirror, desk, or even make it your screen saver! Take it with you by placing it on the dashboard of your car. Keep it in your purse, or use it as a bookmark. When you see the card, recite the verse to yourself with thoughts of your husband.
- This can be a very powerful exercise to help train your mind. You will get as much out of this exercise as you put into it!

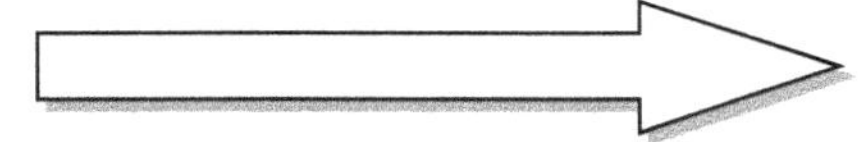

DAILY HOMEWORK

Redirecting your thought life involves daily training with action! You literally have to put new and improved thoughts into your mind in order to have a thought life that produces good fruit. In addition to daily prayer, Bible reading and the three-by-five card with the words from Philippians 4:8, you will record statements that you can say to your husband on a daily basis. This section of the lesson is the most important.

The Daily Homework section is what will really make the difference in you and your marriage! **After you have spoken the positive statement to your husband on each day you should record the date.**

Day one) Record a positive ***true*** statement.

Day two) Record a ***noble*** statement.

Day three) Record a ***right*** statement.

Day four) Record a ***pure*** statement.

Day five) Record a ***lovely*** statement.

Day six) Record an ***admirable*** statement.

Day seven) Record an ***excellent*** or ***praiseworthy*** statement.

DIARY

- ✓ Evaluate and record where you are in your thought life now that you have spent at least one week doing this type of homework:

- ✓ Record any positive comments made to you by your husband, family or friends as a result of working diligently on your personal thought life:

- ✓ How has God personally ministered to you through this study?

Notes

Lesson Two

Blessings

Before the curse, before obedience or disobedience; before *God breathed the breath of life into the nostrils of man*, God blessed man. We were created by God to receive blessings! All people want to be blessed with good health, prosperity and even happiness. Even individuals who don't have a relationship with the Lord will acknowledge they have been "blessed" at certain times in their lives. Whether we know Him or not, the fact remains that we actually crave God's blessings in our lives, you could even say we were wired to receive blessings from God.

Have you ever considered blessings as a real part of marriage? In fact, most weddings will have a blessing as part of the ceremony. Most couples want and recognize their need for God's blessing on their marriage. Not only does God bless our marriage relationship but we can bless each other as husband and wife!

Let's *recapture* some basic truths from Scripture about blessings and their particular significance in our lives.

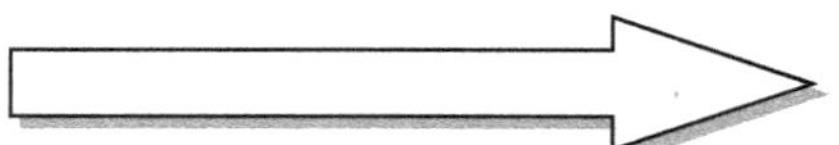

RECAPTURE

I will bless those who bless you, and whoever curses you I will curse; and all the peoples on earth will be blessed through you. Genesis 12:3

This is part of the covenant that God initiated with Abraham from Genesis 12:1-3. Christians have been grafted into this covenant promise through faith in the Lord Jesus Christ. The principle of *God blessing those who bless us* is a real aspect of our everyday lives that we probably don't think about very often. When we say, "God bless you" to someone, are we really conscious of this very principle in action, or are we just saying something that sounds nice and may even be just part of a farewell?

To *recapture* truth about biblical blessings, we are going to do some digging. You will go back in time and look up and record: *first* blessings, *types* of blessings, and how you can *put yourself in a position* to be blessed.

- **Read** all of Genesis chapter one for a foundation for this section of study.

First Blessings

- Record Genesis 1:22

- Record Genesis 1:28

- We immediately see from our very foundation that God has blessed all of creation; from the waters to the dry land, the two bright lights, the vegetation, and the living creatures. After blessing the man and the woman, God gave instructions. What were the instructions from verse 28?

1. ______________________
2. ______________________
3. ______________________
4. ______________________
5. ______________________

We understand from Genesis 1:28 that blessings come with responsibilities. Think about this: when was the last time you counted your blessings and considered the responsibilities that were attached? Take some time and really ponder the totality of this question.

- If you are alive, you have blessings in your life! Consider them now and **record** a few *blessings* that come to mind. Then **record** *responsibilities* you might have regarding these blessings:

Blessings **Responsibilities**

- **Read** Genesis 26:1-14. Now **record** Genesis 26:3.

Types of Blessings

God told Isaac that He would bless him, and promised Isaac and his descendants *"all these lands."* Isaac would need to put himself in a *position* to be blessed.

- How would Isaac do that from verse 3a?

- Have you ever thought about the fact that you can actually place yourself in a position to be blessed by God through obedience to His word?

In verses 12, 13, and 14 you can read how God abundantly blessed Isaac through his obedience by sojourning in the land God chose, instead of going down to Egypt, *"So Isaac stayed in Gera."* Genesis 26:6.

- Why would God fulfill the promise made to Abraham (verse 5)?

There are *responsibilities* attached to blessings. In addition, you have noted that you can put yourself in a *position* to be blessed as well. From what you have learned from verse 3 and verse 5:

- How do you put yourself in a position for God to bless you?

"Instant obedience is the only kind of obedience there is, for delayed obedience is disobedience. Each time God calls upon us to do something, He is offering to make a covenant with us. Our part is to obey, and then He will do His part to send a special blessing."

~ Messages for the Morning Watch *Streams In The Desert*

- In light of what we learned from verse 3 and verse 5, evaluate yourself on how well you are placing yourself in a position to receive all the blessings God has for you. On a scale 1-5 (Five being the greatest), rate how well you:

  Obey God (In a general way)

  1 2 3 4 5

  Keep God's requirements (Specific words of exhortation)

  1 2 3 4 5

  Keep God's commandments (Specific commandments)

  1 2 3 4 5

- Overall, are you in a position to receive all the blessings God wants to bless you with based on what you have learned from this study?

Spiritual Blessings

- For a different type of blessing, **read** Ephesians 1:1-14. Now **record** Ephesians 1:3.

- We don't just have blessings that are physical in nature; we have blessings that are *spiritual* in nature as well! From verse 3, how do you put yourself in a position to receive "every spiritual blessing…?"

Now we will consider our *spiritual blessings*. List each blessing from each verse indicated below.

Blessings from God the Father, verses 4-6

vs. 4

vs. 5

vs. 6b

Blessings from God the Son, verses 7-12

vs. 7a

vs. 7b

vv. 8-10

vv. 11-12

Blessings from God the Holy Spirit, verses 13-14

vs. 13

vs. 14

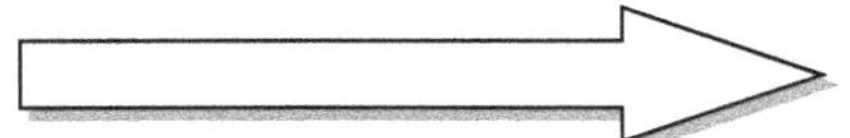

RECONNECT

After such a lengthy study in the *Recapture* section on blessings, you are ready to search out how important blessing your husband is. You will connect what you learned from the last section of your study to your personal relationship with your husband. You will look at specific ways a wife can bless her husband in her marriage relationship. This is your opportunity to *reconnect* your heart with this tremendous gift that as a godly wife you can bring to your marriage.

When you think about blessings from God, it is important to remember that you don't earn blessings from God. You want to remember that you put yourself in a position to be blessed by God through your obedience. Jesus said in John 14:15 "If you love me, you will obey what I command."

- Just think about this: *When was the last time you thought about blessing your husband or being a blessing to him in general?* **Record your thoughts:**

- You will now pull **three blessings** from your **last section** of study and relate them to your husband.

- From Ephesians 1:4, we read that we were "chosen by Him." Think about what that means to you to know that you were chosen. Doesn't that make you feel incredibly special? Now travel back in time—this is your question: Why did you *choose* your husband? Take your time and ask God to remind you of what those reasons were.

- From Ephesians 1:6b we read that we are "accepted in the beloved," (King James Version is best for this verse). This verse relates the fact that we as Christ's beloved don't need to earn His acceptance; He has accepted us once and for all. We all want to be accepted don't we? This is your question: Does your husband feel *accepted* by you, or do you think he may feel that he constantly needs to seek your acceptance? Take your time with this; ask God to help you accurately access the truth.

- From Ephesians 1:7b we read that we "have the forgiveness of sins." What does it mean to you to know that God has forgiven you of all your sins? Sometimes people struggle with past sins feeling the constant weight or even the consequences of old sins. The truth is, "If we confess our sins, He is faithful and just and will forgive us our sins..." I John 1:9. This is your question: Are you holding onto issues of forgiveness regarding your husband?

> "A generous man will prosper; he who refreshes others will himself be refreshed."
> Proverbs 11:25

- **Look up** and **record dictionary definitions for**:
  - Choose
  - Accepted
  - Forgiven

Something to think about: God is the only One who can give us these blessings in the spiritual realm. You are the only one in your marriage relationship who can give these types of blessings to your husband!

- From those three words; which one would bless your husband the most to hear you speak to him?

- Would he be surprised to hear you speak that word to him? If so, explain why here:

"She brings him good, not harm, all the days of her life."
Proverbs 31:12

Chosen, *accepted*, and *forgiven*. These are the hallmarks of our faith, and they should be the hallmarks of your marriage! While doing the little things is important to your marriage relationship, there is nothing more important than practicing these three biblical truths every day of your life.

If you recognize that you have been withholding blessing your husband in these three key areas you should take quick action!

"Now that you know these things, you will be blessed if you do them."
John 13:17

> "If we can open our mouths to talk, we have the ability to communicate the blessing by spoken words. By deciding to communicate words of love and acceptance verbally, we do not have to send away a child, spouse or friend in need."
>
> ~ John Trent
> and
> ~ Gary Smalley
> *The Blessing*

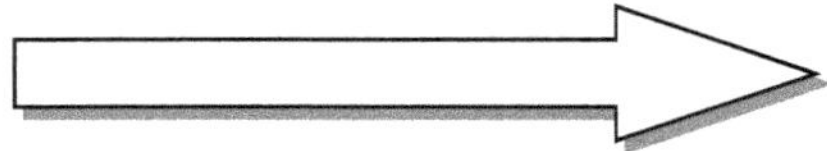

REDIRECT

This section of the lesson will pull together the thoughts and themes from the other two sections by offering practical suggestions with daily homework.

Remember the theme verse on the very first page? "I will bless those who bless you, and whoever curses you I will curse…" Genesis 12:3 (NIV). Isn't it amazing that God will actually bless those we bless? *We have the words, and He has the power!*

You have become aware through your study where blessings come from; who receives them, different types of blessings, and how important it is to put yourself in a position for God to bless you.

This is how it relates to your marriage: Sometimes women get confused about what it means to bless their husbands. They may feel a blessing has to be earned. Or, if they are struggling with issues of forgiveness they may feel justified in withholding blessing their husband. There may even be a thinly veiled attitude of superiority!

Let's be reminded again: Before the curse, before obedience or disobedience; before *God breathed the breath of life into the nostrils of man,* God blessed man!

Blessings literally mean *the gift of God's grace*. We can also be the bearers of the gift of grace. Perhaps you are in a place right now where you see your need to take immediate action, but you don't know where to begin. There is an excellent example in Scripture that gives us a step by step look at what to do.

➢ **Read John 13:1-5**.

- Before Jesus washed the feet of His disciples, He poured water into the basin.

- Before Jesus poured water into the basin, He girded Himself with a towel.

- Before Jesus girded Himself with a towel, He laid aside His garments.

The phrase "laid aside" in the Greek means to *strip yourself*. To *strip yourself,* is the same as laying down your own will. In prayer, acknowledge your willingness to lay down your own will. If you struggle with blessing your husband, confess your struggle, and then ask God to give you a new vision of what blessing your husband will look like. Now expect God to respond to this sincere prayer!

Note the date here:

"…God keeps nothing for Himself. From eternity God had His only begotten Son, and the Father gave Him all things, and nothing that God had was kept back. God is love."

~ Andrew Murray
Absolute Surrender

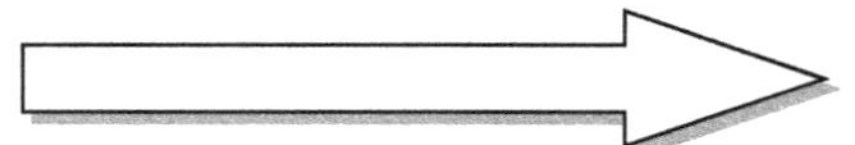

DAILY HOMEWORK

Redirecting your heart will take conscious initiative on your part. In addition to your daily Bible reading and prayer, you will **actively ask God for a *new vision* of what blessing** your husband will look like. Make a point to pray daily asking the Lord to literally bless your husband.

Don't get too technical in this section; the idea is to get yourself thinking in ways that will bless your husband.

Record expressions of blessings for each day of the week. Once you have shared the statement (with/about) your husband please make note of the date.

Day one) Record an expression of how you have *chosen* your husband.

Day two) Record an expression of how you *accept* your husband.

Day three) Record an expression of how you have *forgiven* your husband (Where applicable).

Day four) Record an expression that communicates to your husband your desire to *bless* him and be a blessing to him.

Day five) Record an expression about your husband that can be spoken to: your children, family members, or *mutual* friends that would be a *blessing* to your husband.

Day six) Record an expression that will *bless* your husband regarding his marital commitment to you.

Day seven) Record an expression that will *bless* your husband regarding your marital commitment to him.

DIARY

- ✓ Evaluate and record what blessing your husband looks and feels like now that you have spent at least one week doing this type of homework:

- ✓ Record any positive comments made to you by your husband, family or friends as a result of working diligently on being a blessing to your husband:

- ✓ How has God personally ministered to you through this study?

Notes

Lesson Three

Your Body is Not Your Own

Sometimes marital intimacy can become the big white elephant in the room that no one wants to talk about but everyone is thinking about! Marital intimacy can be one of the most struggled over facets of marriage. The devil has had a lot of success in tearing down this special gift that God has created expressly for marriage. While the devil can use this facet of marriage to create problems—God can use it to create strength, peace, and joy!

Marital intimacy can be a touchy subject to tackle. But remember; this is *BOOT CAMP*, and so we will march forward and look at what Scripture has to say about this very important aspect of marriage!

Let's begin to *recapture* truth from Scripture about this very intimate subject matter. We may be surprised to discover how much Scripture actually has to say on the subject!

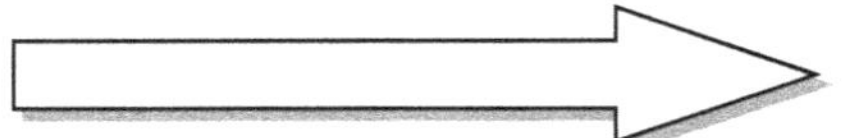

RECAPTURE

The wife's body does not belong to her alone but also to her husband. In the same way, the husband's body does not belong to him alone but also to his wife.1Corinthians 7:4

In this chapter of 1 Corinthians, Paul takes up the subject of *the big white elephant*! Paul begins this portion of Scripture by saying, "Now for the matters you wrote about..." Even back in *Bible times,* married couples wanted godly guidance for this facet of marriage. They had real questions and Paul gave real answers! Sexual relations in marriage are important and Paul gave the subject its due weight. Paul couldn't have addressed this issue more directly than he did in this very passage of Scripture!

✝ For a foundation you will **read** 1 Corinthians 7:1-5. Before you read these verses, would you please pause and pray right now sincerely asking the Lord to give you a willing heart to be ministered to.

From **verse 2,** what are you told each man/woman should *have*?

From **verse 3,** what are you told husbands/wives should *do*?

From **verse 4,** what are you told about your body?

From **verse 5,** what are you told *not* to do?

From **verse 5,** what is the *exception*?

There is nothing complicated about this instruction from Paul about marriage. This instruction is about as straight forward as it gets!

Let's do a word study on each key word found in these verses to enhance appreciation for the instructions given. Use your **dictionary to look up** and **record definitions** for:

- own
- fulfill
- belong
- deprive

"It is not your love that sustains the marriage, but from now on, the marriage that sustains your love."
~ Dietrich Bonhoeffer
Bonhoeffer

- What new appreciation have you gained towards this aspect of marriage just as a result of doing this word study?

Do you struggle with thoughts about your body belonging to your husband? Explain your answer.

- In your own words, explain what it means to you to know that your body belongs to your husband, and that his body belongs to you?

- **Read** and **record** Genesis 2:24.

- Does this verse give you a better understanding about husbands and wives bodies belonging to one another?

- Write Genesis 2:24 in your own words, substituting *man* and *wife* with your own names.

- If you were to ask your husband to respond to each verse from 1 Corinthians 7:1-5, how do you think he would respond? Circle yes or no.

Verse 3: My wife fulfills her marital duty.

Yes/No

Verse 4: My wife understands her body is not her own.

Yes/No

Verse 5: My wife has deprived me of marital intimacies.

Yes/No

- How does this make you feel?

"...It may surprise you to learn that many people have affairs not because they are drooling with uncontrolled passions, but because for the first time in their lives someone has come along and made them feel significant during a time when they especially needed it."

~ Joseph M. Stowell

Perilous Pursuits

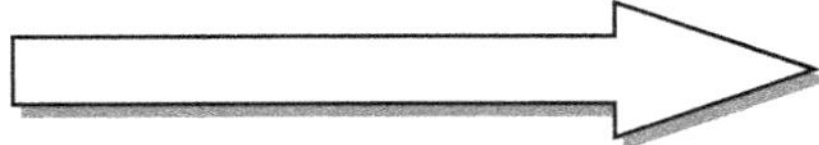

RECONNECT

You read from 1 Corinthians 7:5 that married couples are not to *deprive* one another. The Amplified Bible reads, "Do not *refuse* and *deprive* and *defraud* each other [of your due marital rights]... " In other words, sexual relations are yours as a right of marriage. It is even expected!

Sometimes in a struggling marriage couples don't appreciate the healing power of sexual relations. And the devil knows this! This is truth: sometimes things that mattered before – don't matter quite as much after sexual relations. Marital intimacy can soften hearts; attitudes, words, and actions.

- Have you ever thought about that exhortation in this way: If you refuse marital intimacies, you are depriving not just your husband or yourself, but you are depriving your marriage in general?

From verse 5 we are told that there should be agreement between the husband and the wife when to abstain from sexual relations. There is ebb and flow that married couples can experience in their intimate relationship. There is also a difference between couples experiencing a "dry spell" during their marriage due to schedules, illness, and the like; rather than one partner or the other withholding sexual relations for their own reasons. This is the bottom line: husbands and wives do know the difference between the two!

"Drink water from your own cistern, running water from your own well."
Proverbs 5:15

- From verse 5, what did Paul say could happen if married couples did deprive one another of this right of marriage?

- Share as many examples as you can think of as to how Satan could tempt either husbands or wives if they deprived one another of this right of marriage.

There is a principle of liberty that Paul speaks about in 1 Corinthians 8 that we should consider now, *never cause a weaker brother to stumble*. For example: in the marriage relationship, if the wife is depriving her husband, it may not necessarily cause her to stumble, but she could cause her own husband to stumble.

- **Read** and **record** 1 Corinthians 8:9.

- Paul is so emphatic that Christians should *not cause a brother (or sister) to stumble,* that he concludes his statement with these words from verse 13. What are they?

"He who works his land will have abundant food, but he who chases fantasies lacks judgment."
Proverbs 12:11

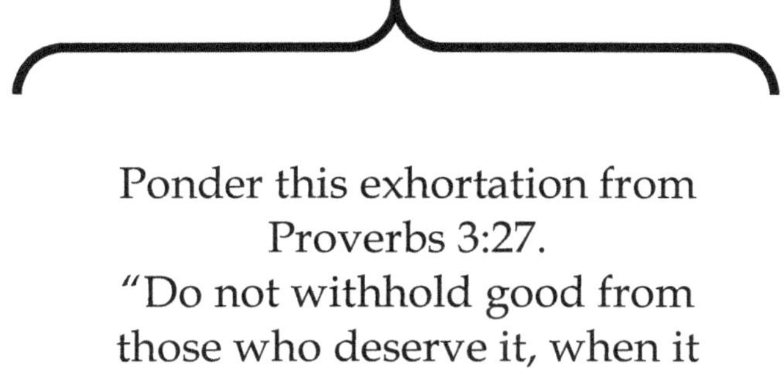

Ponder this exhortation from Proverbs 3:27.
"Do not withhold good from those who deserve it, when it is in *your power to act.*"

Paul was willing to never eat meat again in order to keep a brother from stumbling. What are you willing *to never do again*, if it would potentially cause your *husband* to stumble? Before you answer, consider this: Paul's love and commitment to Jesus Christ was the basis for his passion towards the brethren, and these are men and women that he had not taken vows with!

Some women who withhold marital intimacies from their husbands don't consider the real temptation they are allowing their husbands to go through. (While there is no excuse for infidelities of any kind, you never want to be a willing participant for your husband to be tempted in this way).

- If you have been guilty of non-biblical sexual deprivation in your marriage, do you still feel justified? If so, explain your reason here:

- If you answered yes to the above question, what does God have to say to you through this lesson? (Also recall your last lesson on Blessings: *Chosen, Accepted* and *Forgiven*)

- From this passage of Scripture, Paul is really warning the church to not forfeit their liberty. From 1 Corinthians 10:12, what is Paul's specific warning?

In the Genesis record we are told that sexual relations are good. It has already been noted that Satan has done his best to distort healthy and godly sexual relations. Some people have been hurt by the inappropriate use and practice of sexual relations.

The beauty of our God is that He is bigger than all our hurts and wounds! Corrie Ten Boom, a Nazi Concentration Camp survivor, has said, "There is no pit too deep, that He is not deeper still!" Amen! Remember God's plans for you from Jeremiah 29:11 from your first lesson? They are: *to prosper you, to give you a hope, to give you a future*! God does not want any of His children to live a depleted life as a result of someone else's sin!

If you are someone who has been hurt in this way, it is important to find one person you can trust, who will be a confident and who will pray with you. Be very choosy as to whom this person might be. Look for a mature woman in Christ, one who does not gossip, who is compassionate and is also able to give biblical insights.

Sometimes women get involved in sexual relations before they are married, and sometimes even at a very young age. This can have devastating consequences on the woman as she gets older. She may not even realize that her prior sexual relations are at the root of her own problems in her current marriage.

The principle of becoming one through sexual relations is real. God made it that way. So if a woman has been joined with other men, she needs to take that to the cross of Christ, repent, and receive forgiveness and cleansing.

➢ Read 1 John 1:9.

✝ What does it very personally say to you?

How can I tell the difference between conviction of sin by the Holy Spirit and condemnation of sin by Satan? Condemnation leaves you hopeless where you see no way out or any other future. Conviction of sin leaves you hopeful knowing there is forgiveness and steps that can be taken to get back on track.

✝ The baggage of old sins can weigh you down and complicate your life, but what does **Romans 8:1** say?

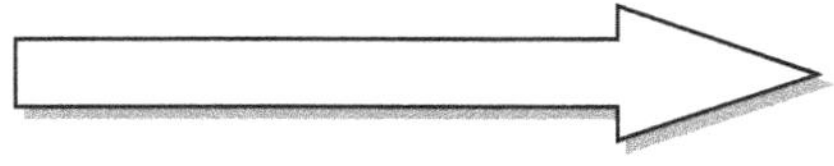

REDIRECT

This section of the lesson will pull together thoughts and themes from the other two sections by offering practical suggestions with daily homework.

This is something to think about: women are all about words—while men are all about action! Do you realize sexual relations in marriage are a form of communication? I don't think women in particular think about sexual relations being a type of communication in their marriage. Women want words, while most men want action. If women would understand that sexual relations are just another form of communication by their husbands, they might not be so suspicious of their husband's motives and become stingy with their energies regarding this aspect of marriage.

Something to think about: Your husband just wants to tell you that he loves you!

Men and women do think differently, and we often have different approaches to the same subject. That's okay, it's even good. You married a man—enjoy the way he has been uniquely created! If you struggle with your husband's motives for desiring your affections, this might be a new and insightful thought for you. He just wants to tell you that he loves you!

- Some women may need to re-think their husband's motives regarding this aspect of marriage. *Could this be you?*

- Some women may need to humble themselves in the sight of the Lord and acknowledge to Him that they have not been a willing wife. *Could this be you?*

- Some women may need to humble themselves in the sight of their husband and this may be much harder to do. If you have deprived your husband for non-biblical reasons, you should pray about how you can apologize, and ask for your husband's forgiveness. *Could this be you?*

"...Today, if you hear his voice,
do not harden your hearts."
Hebrews 7:4

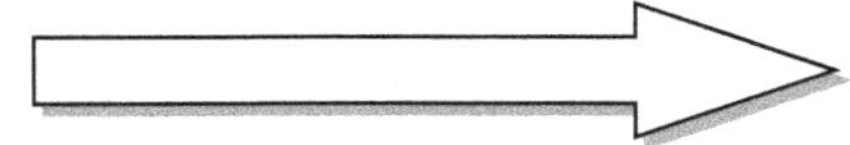

DAILY HOMEWORK

Redirecting your attitude and actions regarding marital intimacy can be difficult. Let me share a personal story first: Many years ago when our son was very little, my husband and I were having a little "dry spell." Not feeling good about this, I asked the Lord what I could do. God simply inspired me to go outside where my husband was working on a sprinkler line and just put my arms around his neck and tell him that I loved him. It was so simple! God knew exactly how I could ignite this aspect of our marriage.

If you are struggling in this area, you may not know where to begin, but God does! Pray, ask the Lord to help you. This will be the most important part of this lesson. If you approach this homework with a sincere heart, you will be putting yourself in a position for God to help you. The key is your *sincere* heart!

Once you have completed the homework for each day please date it. This is your daily homework:

Day one) If you are a woman who struggles with the marital instructions in 1 Corinthians

7, how can 2 Timothy 3:16 help you? Whether you struggle or not, please record 2 Timothy 3:16 and your thoughts.

Day two) Record a prayer here. This could be a prayer for forgiveness, or it could be a prayer for a heart to even be willing to see your need for forgiveness in this area of your marriage. If this is not a problem in your marriage, write a prayer to God for you and your husband to remain attentive to this aspect of your marriage.

Day three) Record a prayer which asks God to show you a way to ignite this aspect of your marriage with new insights.

Day four) Record thoughts you have or ideas the Lord may have given you. (These could be practical in nature or simply thoughts of the heart).

Day five) Record how you are *feeling* now that you are praying for this specific area of your marriage.

Day six) Perspective is everything. Please read all of 1 Corinthians 13 now, particularly verse 5. Also note, *three things remain; but one is the greatest,* which is it, and why is this perspective important in your intimate marriage relationship?

Day seven) If this aspect of your marriage has become a matter of real prayer for you; today, prayerfully consider asking your husband to partner in prayer with you about this.

DIARY

- ✓ Evaluate and record your thoughts about this aspect of your marriage now that you have been doing this type of homework for at least one week:

- ✓ Record any positive comments made to you by your husband as a result of diligently working on this aspect of your marriage, or perhaps, you may have noticed a change in his general demeanor.

- ✓ How has God personally ministered to you through this study?

Notes

Lesson Four

The Submissive Wife, Get Real!

Many women, including Christian women, struggle with this aspect of marriage. The role of the woman in marriage can be so misunderstood! Television, magazines, and even radio all help to undermine this biblical principle. Many women have the perception that a submissive wife is a woman who has become a doormat having no rights or a voice of her own, and that perspective is far from true biblical submission! In fact, it is a deceitful lie which robs many marriages from experiencing true harmony!

I recall one Sunday morning's message being on the topic of the role of the wife, in particular her submission to her husband. After the service my grandmother leaned over and whispered in my ear, "I always had trouble with that part." I got a good laugh while appreciating her honesty! Maybe you can relate?

Perspective is everything. Hasn't it been your experience that once you understand why you are to do something it changes your attitude by giving you proper perspective? How many times in your life's experience have you said, "Now I get it, yes, I can do that!"? This lesson will reveal the heart of the submissive wife by examining her perspective in a way that maybe you haven't thought of before.

Let's *recapture* truth from Scripture about this often misunderstood aspect of marriage for wives.

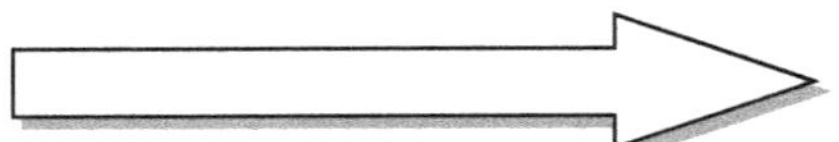

RECAPTURE

For this is the way the holy women of the past who put their hope in God used to make themselves beautiful. They were submissive to their own husbands. 1 Peter 3:5

Remember who is writing this word of instruction? It's Peter! Peter is one man in Scripture who really learned the hard way, he's just so relatable! Immediately we first note Peter's tender approach to this subject. In this passage Peter doesn't just tell wives what to do; he also explains what the results can be which helps give women perspective, and that can make all the difference!

➢ **Read** all of 1 Peter 3 now for a foundation.

1. From verse 1, who is Peter addressing?

2. From verse 1, who are wives to submit?

3. From verse 1, what can be the result of submitting to your husband?

From our last lesson, we acknowledged that most women are all about words—while most men are all about action. This passage of Scripture really seems to make that point; many women do struggle with words! In 1 Peter 3:1 we are told husbands *may be won over without words*. Imagine that, won over without words! That might be a new perspective for many women.

With that thought in mind, let's begin a word study. **Look up** and **record dictionary definitions** for:

- Submissive

- Won

- Without

- Behavior

- Being as truthful as possible with yourself, what thoughts came to mind as you were in the process of this word study?

- Being as truthful as possible with yourself, from your own experience as a married woman and in general, have your words mostly helped or hurt your marriage? Explain your answer:

✝ For more perspective, let's study the "why" for being a submissive wife. **Review** verses 5 and 6 now.

1. From verse 5, who are the examples Christian women are to follow?

2. From verse 5, who did these women put their hope in?

3. From verse 5, what did their godly behavior produce?

4. From verse 6, by name, who is the example of a godly woman?

5. From verse 6, who are you if you do what is right?

6. From verse 6, what are you to *not give way to?*

SARAH *"Princess"*

Peter could have used any number of women from the Old Testament as an example of a holy and submissive wife, but he chose Sarah as the example! A much humbler and more mature Peter defers to a woman not unlike himself. Both had to learn biblical truths the hard way!

When you study the life of Sarah from the Genesis record, you realize she was not always the woman that is described in 1 Peter chapter three. Sarah was often strong willed; she definitely was a woman of words, and there was even a moment when she doubted the very word of God. Sound familiar? Peter suffered as a result of the very same mistakes! Thousands of years separated these two individuals, but they were definitely kindred spirits!

And so, this is our hope—Sarah is our example! That gives all of the strong willed women of God hope, and one more perspective!

- Let's read about this strong willed woman who is remembered in the New Testament as a submissive wife. **Read** all of **Genesis 16** now.

1. From verse 2, how did Abraham respond to Sarah's words?

2. From verse 5, how did Sarah respond to Abraham after he did what she wanted him to do?

3. From verse 5, did Sarah take any responsibility for their present situation?

4. From verse 16, who was born to Abraham?

- From this story of Sarah, how do you feel about her?

- Do you identify with any of her traits or actions?

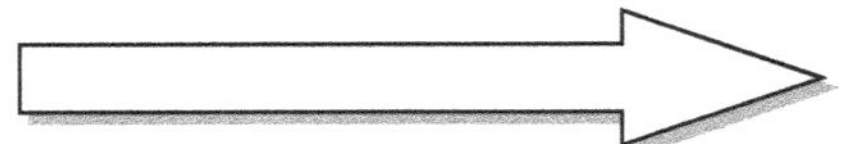

RECONNECT

In this section we will work at aligning our hearts with true biblical submission, in a real way!

It's true, even godly women struggle with this aspect of biblical marriage. They can also discover they may have been deceived, which may be an enlightening perspective! For example: A godly woman may agree with Scripture, but at the same time be so disconnected with really applying this Word of God to her life, that she doesn't even know that she's not! That's called deception!

It is very important that women of God receive this exhortation seriously, and give it due weight. Ponder this truth in Obadiah 1:3, *"The pride of your heart has deceived you."* Sometimes we can be deceived, and sometimes we can deceive ourselves!

Let's do some digging and see what Scripture has to say about deception. This may be a new perspective for you as it relates to understanding the role of the submissive wife!

Self-deception

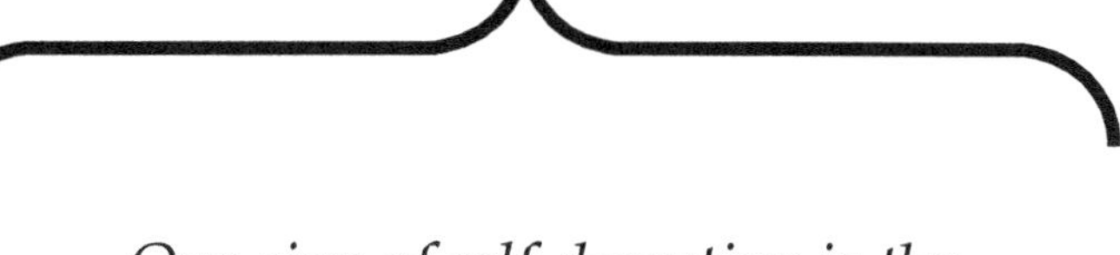

One sign of self-deception is the thought that you are always right. This can be really hard to evaluate in yourself, because you will always agree with yourself! Please pause right now and pray that the Holy Spirit will speak truth, open the understanding of your heart, and reveal to you whether or not you are someone who is deceived.

- **Read** and **record** 1 John 1:8

We often hear people say, "Oh, I know I'm not perfect, I know I'm a sinner." They may say that because they know that is the right thing to say. But if that person can't point to specific sins and wrong doings, they are deceived! There is a difference between a person who says that they *know* they are a sinner as a general statement, and the person who can *point* to specific sins they have committed!

- Are you able to point to specific sins you have committed, calling the sin what it is? Share your thoughts.

- **Read** and **record** Genesis 16:3

"The wise woman builds her house, but with her own hands the foolish one tears hers down."
Proverbs 14:1

Sarah took a souvenir from Egypt, her name was Hagar. Sarah believed that God had prevented her from having children of her own, so she devised a plan. Sarah's plan was worldly. It's interesting to note she used a woman who came from a land that is also biblically representative of the world. God didn't tell Sarah to do this, and neither did Abraham suggest it. It was Sarah's own idea. Sarah was a woman who deceived herself!

- Have you ever devised a plan expecting God to bless it, and later realized that you had only deceived yourself with the thought that it was a plan God could bless? If yes, explain your answer. Were there consequences?

God has given women the ability to powerfully persuade their husbands. It is important that we don't abuse our persuasive powers. "Abraham listened to the voice of Sarah." Managing your ability to persuade your husband responsibly is another form of submission. One more perspective!

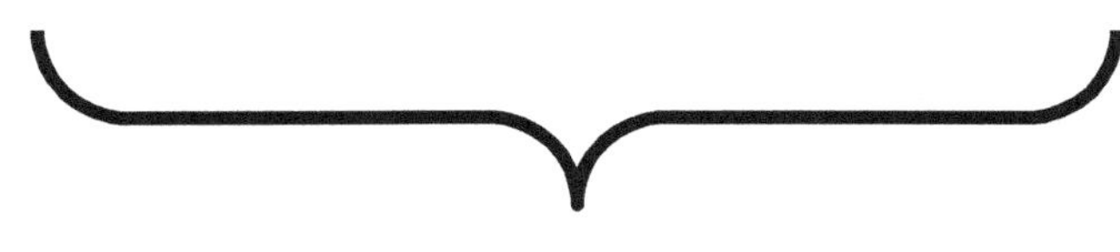

What's the connection between deception and the importance of biblical submission? Protection! Our husbands are appointed and anointed as our protectors! If Sarah would have been submissive to Abraham by patiently waiting with him for God to fulfill His promise and had not manipulated Abraham with her words, she would have been protected from her plan which eventually cost not only them, but generations to come, so greatly!

Deception from Satan

There is another notable woman who was deceived in Scripture, her name is Eve. You know the story; she was tempted by none other than Satan himself. While there are many applications from that story, the bottom line is that Eve was deceived, and as a result she influenced Adam to sin along with her.

Satan's only purpose for deception is to ruin you. Satan wants to see God's people fail! And you don't want any part of his demonic deceptive plans. Even if your husband is not a Christian, God can still use your husband to protect you as you hide under his protective covering. God always honors His own order. We see the immediate—while God sees into eternity. You can trust that God knows how to direct your husband, even in apparent failure. And that's what biblical submission really is, trusting God!

"God's Word doesn't promise us that we will be victorious over sin and death. Rather, it says with all its might that someone has won this victory, and that this person, if we have him as Lord, will also win the victory over us."

~ Dietrich Bonhoeffer

Words To Die For

- The apostle Paul gives one more perspective about how Eve was deceived by Satan. **Read** and **record** 2 Corinthians 11:3.

- How did Satan deceive Eve in 2 Corinthians 11:3?

- When Satan deceives, what happens to your mind?

- Paul adds perspective to this thought as he relates to young Timothy the importance of women not having authority over men. **Read** and **record** 1 Timothy 2:14.

- Who was not deceived?

- Who was the first sinner?

"If you have played the fool and exalted yourself, or if you have planned evil, clap your hand over your mouth!"
Proverbs 30:32

It's important to understand that Paul is not in any way suggesting that women are stupid, but rather Satan is the master manipulator, and he knew how to manipulate Eve's understanding through powerful deceiving suggestions. It was Eve herself who told God that she had been deceived in Genesis 3:13. If Eve hadn't been deceived, she would never have eaten the forbidden fruit!

- Is it possible that you are being deceived today? Explain your answer either way.

- After reading, recording, and studying, explain in your own words how deception can be used to undermine biblical submission.

Removing Deception

Perspective can be twisted if we have been deceived or are deceiving ourselves. Let's begin the process of removing layers of **possible deception!**

- What word is the opposite of deception?
- From John 8:32, what are you told about truth?
- From John 14:6, *Who* is the truth?
- Is there an area of disobedience that could be contributing to deceptive thoughts in your life? If so, record your thoughts here.
- If there is an area of disobedience in which you have felt the conviction of the Lord, are you willing today to let go of what holds you, and obey His best for you? If so, record your thoughts and the date here.
- What does 2 Corinthians 11:14 say?

There is only one source of truth, and that is the Holy One as He is revealed through His Holy Word. Women who are suspicious and have trouble trusting Holy Scripture are prone to deception. However, it has been said by someone, "You can trust the Man who died for you!"

- How important is it to know, understand, and appropriate the Word of God in your life in light of what 2 Corinthians 11:14 states about Satan's deceptions?

If you struggle with discerning real truth, read what Oswald Chambers has to say: *"If there is something upon which God has put His pressure, obey in that matter, bring your imagination into captivity to the obedience of Christ with regard to it and everything will become as clear as daylight. The tiniest thing we allow in our lives that is not under the control of the Holy Spirit is quite sufficient to account for spiritual muddle, and all the thinking we like to spend on it will never make it clear. Spiritual muddle is only made plain by obedience. Immediately we obey, we discern."*

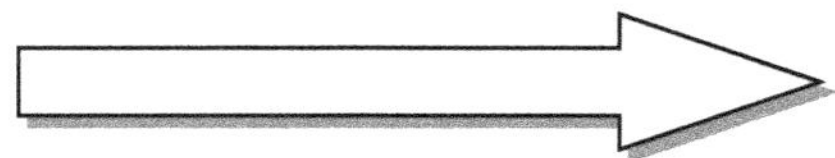

REDIRECT

This section of the lesson will pull together the thoughts and themes from the other two sections by offering practical suggestions with daily homework.

"...In the end it was decided to send a distant connection of the family named Pride....It was emphasized that if no other means proved unsuccessful he was to feel no scruples against exerting all his powers of fascination in order to coax Much-Afraid away from the Shepherd"

~Hannah Hurnard

Hinds' Feet On High Places

Do you struggle trusting that the Lord is able to honor His Word as you obey it? Could this be your perspective right now? If you recognize today that you are holding back and holding on, will you prayerfully lay your trust at the feet of Jesus, who loves you so much?

This could be another perspective: Listen to what Jesus told the religious leaders who were questioning Him from John 8:47, *"He who is of God hears the words of God: for this reason you do not hear them, because you are not of God."* If you struggle with receiving truth from the Bible, could it be possible that you are not of God?

Sometimes there is more to a stubborn heart than what meets the eye. The root of deception can also be disbelief. There is a remedy, the very Word of Truth Himself, Jesus Christ the Lord.

Jesus loves you! And He wants you to experience all that He has for you—love, peace, and joy! His Word, the Bible, is not just a set of rules to be followed, but it is a love story that will help you get to know Him very personally and will give you help with your daily life!

If you are not sure about your salvation but want to be sure, simply stop and pray right now. Tell the Lord that you need Him in your life, and that you recognize you are a sinner in need of a Savior. Don't waste one more minute not being sure of your salvation. If you have prayed this type of prayer, you can be sure! It is also good to tell someone who is a Christian what you have done, they will rejoice with you.

"Everyone who calls upon the name of the Lord will be saved." Romans 10:13

DAILY HOMEWORK

Redirecting your attitude and actions as a submissive wife has much to do with understanding the heart of submission. This is the easiest perspective to grasp on this subject, you are simply *pleasing* your husband! Every wife knows what her husband likes. For example: One husband might want his wife to take charge of all the household finances, and that looks like submission to him. Another husband might want his wife to let go of the household finances, and that looks like submission to him.

You will record specific acts of submission as they relate to your husband. After you have completed each day's assignment, please record the date.

Day one) My husband would be pleased if I let go of…

Day two) My husband would be pleased if I did…

Day three) My husband would be pleased if I said…

Day four) My husband would be pleased if I stopped saying…

Day five) If you have children, would they say you are a submissive wife? How does this make you feel?

Day six) Commit in prayer to God your desire to be a biblically submissive wife, record the date here. Note: If you are not willing to take time today and pray this prayer, also record the date.

Day seven) Share with your husband your desire to please him in a way that he will know is sincere and communicates a submissive heart.

DIARY

- ✓ Evaluate and record how you feel about being a biblically submissive wife after doing this type of homework for at least one week.

- ✓ Record any positive comments made to you by your husband, family, or friends as a result of working diligently on being a submissive wife.

- ✓ How has God personally ministered to you through this study?

Notes

Lesson Five

Raise the Bar and Don't Cross Those Lines

Women are aware of how important it is to show respect to other people by not crossing certain "lines" that can hurt or anger another person. There are basic areas that can be considered off limits in all relationships, and most women understand what those areas are, especially as it relates to the marriage relationship.

Sometimes in the marriage relationship couples will cross those "lines" out of a lack of respect, or for the intentional purpose to either anger or hurt the other marriage partner. It can also be used as a *weapon of war* in marriage to gain a feeling of superiority. This is so destructive to any relationship, but especially the marriage relationship! This type of behavior creates antagonism, distrust, and closes down communication quicker than most anything else can!

Through this lesson you will study how you can "raise the bar" of your personal integrity, and the importance of not "crossing lines" in all relationships, but especially in your marital relationship!

Let's *recapture* truths from Scripture about how important personal integrity really can be, even in the most difficult situations.

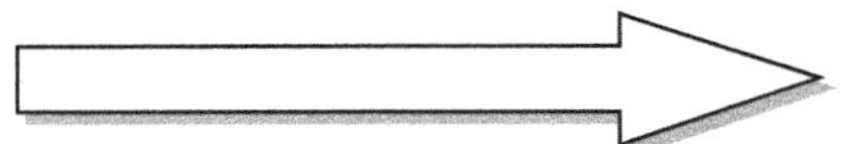

RECAPTURE

"...the Lord forbid that I should do such a thing to my master, the Lord's anointed, or lift my hand against him; for he is the anointed of the Lord." 1 Samuel 24:6

David is one individual who successfully handled a situation that could have had devastating consequences had he not chosen to "raise the bar and not cross those lines!" David had every opportunity at this moment in his life to right wrongs and to achieve apparent success in the battle between himself and King Saul. You will discover not only that David maintained his own personal integrity—but that of those who were under his personal leadership!

➢ **Read** all of 1 Samuel 24 now.

Saul was jealous of David and wanted him dead! It could have been so tempting; David definitely had the upper hand in this situation. However this passage of Scripture records one of David's shining moments—a moment that reminds us why David was called *the man after God's own heart!* Not only did David *raise the bar* of integrity for himself, but also for the men who were under his leadership and influence. David was not willing to cross lines that he knew God could not bless! David understood that no matter what, King Saul was still the king and the Lord's anointed!

There is much that can be integrated into a woman's life from this story of personal integrity and *lines* that should not be crossed. In particular to this study, wives will learn about the importance of not crossing lines of disrespect, even when it may appear to justify their position or point of view. Wives will also study the importance of raising the bar in their own personal integrity as it relates to husbands, marriage, and the influence this can have on their own children.

Let's begin to break down this story in relatable sections; you will begin with the facts as they are presented in Scripture.

✝ From verse 4, what did David do?

- From verse 5, how did this make David feel?

- From verse 6, how did David view Saul?

- From verse 7, what did David do for his men?

For the sake of this study, you will now substitute the characters from this passage of Scripture and relate them to your own life. **Who could each character represent?**

Saul ____________________

David ____________________

David's Men ____________________

Word Study

- The robe of Saul was a personal garment which identified him as a king having authority over David. In this story David cut a portion of King Saul's robe off to demonstrate that he had power over Saul in his most vulnerable moment.

Record definitions for:

- Authority

- Vulnerable

- David didn't have a peace about what he had done, he felt bad, even though it seemed like it was the right thing to do at the time. David knew he had crossed the line, "*David's conscience bothered him....*"

Record definitions for:

- Peace

- Fair

- Right

- Conscience

- David was further able to persuade his men to not attack Saul. David's own conviction had a powerful influence on his men, therefore preventing his men from sinning against the Lord.

Record definitions for:

- Persuade

- Attack

- Prevent

RECONNECT

You have already begun the process of integrating the lessons of David's response by substituting yourself with David, your husband with Saul, and your children with the men under David's leadership. You have also completed a word study that analyzes select words to help you understand key points from this story.

Now let's make it personal. Let us align our hearts with basic truths found from verses four through seven as it personally relates to you in your marriage. **You will need to dig deep and be especially honest with yourself for this section of the lesson to bear any fruit!**

Raise the Bar

Pray—and take your time with this section, and allow the Holy Spirit to speak to you.

- From the scenario in verse 4, describe a time when you might have "cut a piece of the robe" (an attitude of disrespect) from your husband?

- How did this make you feel? Did you relate to how David felt from verse 5, or did/do you feel justified?

- Like David from verse 6, did/do you recognize your husband's position in your marriage? Do you relate to the *respect* and *esteem* that David had for Saul in the position that God had placed Saul in?

- If you have children, did/do you persuade your children to respect and esteem their father like David did with his men in verse 7? Or do you teach and allow them to think, speak, and act disrespectfully to their father by your example of behavior and/or words?

Don't Cross those Lines

Pray—and take your time with this section, and allow the Holy Spirit to speak to you.

- **Make a list** that can represent *"lines"* that you should not cross in your marital relationship. (This could be verbal lines; statements or references made that are not appreciated by your husband. This also could be actions; i.e. making purchases or commitments, etc. that you know displease your husband.)

"When a man's ways are pleasing to the LORD, he makes even his enemies live at peace with him."
Proverbs 16:7

- **Review your definitions** from your word study on page 3 from the *Recapture* section. Are there certain words, or is there one word in particular that God is pointing His finger at? Is He speaking to you about something right now? Your willingness to listen to the Lord about any of these areas will benefit your personal integrity and therefore have a huge positive impact on your marriage! **Share your thoughts here.**

"Better to live on a corner of the roof than share a house with a quarrelsome wife."
Proverbs 21:9

- What would *"raise the bar and not crossing those lines"* look like in your marriage? **Dig deep and be specific.**

- Why is the "high bar" of personal integrity so important in marriage?

There is a passage of Scripture in the New Testament that speaks directly to the Christian about their own personal integrity (Philippians 2:1-11). The passage reminds us of some very important heart and mind attitudes that should be cultivated in every believer's life. The attitudes studied from this passage will remain a constant work throughout the believer's life, but, *"being confident of this, that he who began a good work in you will carry it on to completion until the day of Christ Jesus."* Philippians 1:6

> "It's the humble who are perceptive; they're skilled in discerning the work of God in others because they care about others and want to serve others."
>
> ~ C. J. Mahaney
>
> *Humility*

- **Read Philippians 2:1-11 now.**

- There is one word that sums up this passage of Scripture, what is it?

Recalling David and Saul in the cave, it is easy to recognize that *humility* was the motivating force behind David's ability to recognize his heart had crossed lines that it should not have. It was humility that moved David forward, and raised the bar of his own personal integrity and set the example for his men.

✝ Explain how humility can help raise the bar in your personal integrity and therefore raise the bar in your marital relationship?

➢ **Read** and **record Philippians 2:3**

✝ What would happen if you <u>actually</u> did consider your husband *to be better than yourself?*

✝ Now let's make this real! List 10 ways in which you could *consider your husband better than yourself.* (This is within your capabilities! It could be very helpful to review the words from your word study now.)

1.

2.

3.

4.

5.

6.

7.

8.

9.

10.

When you read the words from Philippians 2:3, you immediately see that it is a tall order to fill! It sounds good and you can agree with it, but how do you make it real? The point of this last exercise is to get you to literally *think better of your husband than yourself!*

Some women may think they already do think more highly of their husbands than themselves, but when push comes to shove and they have to record ways in which they *actually* do think more highly of their husbands, they may discover how very short they do come to the high bar that Paul writes about!

"...and the passing of time, and the way you react to that leader—be he David or Saul—reveals a great deal about you."
~ Gene Edwards
A Tale Of Three Kings

- Did you find this exercise difficult or easy to do? Rate your response on a scale of 1-5 (Five being the most difficult).

1 2 3 4 5

- How do you feel about this?

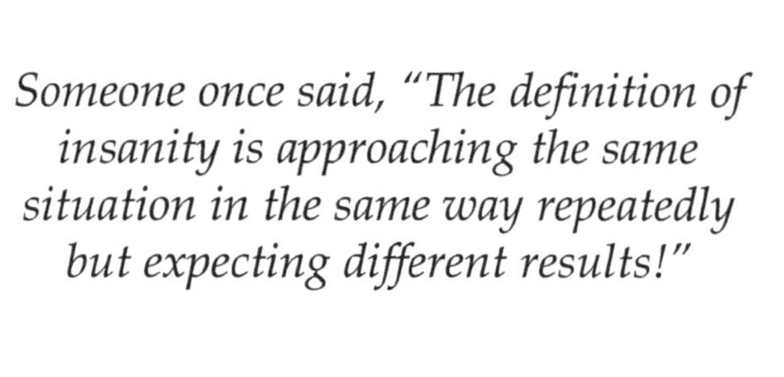

Someone once said, "The definition of insanity is approaching the same situation in the same way repeatedly but expecting different results!"

REDIRECT

This section of the lesson will pull together the thoughts and themes from the other two sections by offering practical suggestions with daily homework:

If you find that you struggle with constantly crossing lines with your husband—you need to raise the bar in your own personal integrity. You may actually think that you are approaching difficult areas of your marriage in different ways, and perhaps on the surface you are. But if you are not seeing results, maybe the problem is that you are approaching the same difficulty with the same *heart* giving you the *heart problem*! A heart that really isn't as sincere as it could be!

Remember, you are in *BOOT CAMP for the Married Woman's Soul*, and so you must be willing to examine your heart, your motives, and the real results that your choices cause you and your husband to live with daily. You must be willing to look at how you approach difficulties in your marriage and how you think about your husband. And if you have children or even grandchildren, what affect does all of this have on them?

Will you prayerfully commit to the Lord your desire to *raise the bar* of your own personal integrity and *not cross those lines* of disrespect?

If you are willing to pray such a prayer, expect God to orchestrate circumstances for you to be tried in these areas, for that is the only way you will know that type work is being done! Record your thoughts:

"…work out your own salvation..."
Philippians 2:12.

Listen to what Oswald Chambers says about this verse:
"You have to work out with concentration and care what God works in; not work your own salvation, but work it out, while you base resolutely in unshaken faith on the complete and perfect Redemption of the Lord.

DAILY HOMEWORK

Redirecting your attitude and actions in *raising the bar* and *not crossing lines* will involve thinking about specific ways that you can accomplish this. This section of the lesson will give you daily opportunities to do just that!

You will write out these specific opportunities and when you have completed each one, whether in heart or deed, please record the date.

Day one) *Heart* attitude: record a ***heart attitude*** you know would help your husband feel supported.

Day two) *Heart* attitude: record a ***heart attitude*** you know would help your husband feel compassion from you.

Day three) *Heart* attitude: record a ***heart attitude*** you know would help your husband feel safe expressing or exposing his vulnerabilities to you.

Day four) *Deed*: record a ***deed*** (words or action) that you can do today that will communicate to your husband your desire to raise the bar in your marriage in a general way.

Day five) *Deed*: record a ***deed*** (words or action) that you can do today that will demonstrate that you will no longer cross a line that you know has displeased your husband.

Day six) *Deed*: record a ***deed*** (words or action) that you can to do today that will demonstrate to your children or grandchildren (if applicable) that you are raising the bar and not willing to cross certain lines anymore.

Day seven) *Deed*: if you have crossed lines, and through this lesson have prayed asking the Lord to help you raise the bar of your own personal integrity, will you apologize to your husband about having crossed certain lines in the past?

DIARY

- ✓ Evaluate your current heart attitude, and record any new perspective(s) you have gained as a result of doing this study.

- ✓ Record any positive comments made to you by your husband, family, or friends as a result of working diligently on raising the bar in your own personal integrity and not crossing lines that you know can displease or disrespect your husband.

- ✓ How has God personally ministered to you through this study?

Notes

Lesson Six

Commitment and Loyalty

Along with love and respect, commitment and loyalty are the most desired traits both men and women want from their marriage partner. Men and women want to know that they can count on one another; each wants the assurance that they will have at least one person in this world that will stand by their side faithfully as long as they shall live!

Sadly, the truth is that commitment and loyalty are not the enduring traits found in many marriages today. Extramarital affairs and divorce continue to be on the rise, including Christian couples—and this ought not to be!

In addition to commitment and loyalty, this lesson will expose a secret many men and women keep throughout their marriage; it's the *opt-out card.* This means one or both partners believe that divorce can be a real option if they want out of their marital commitment. And lastly you will study the importance of *marital fidelity* – mind, heart, and body!

Let's *recapture* truths from Scripture about these important components in marriage.

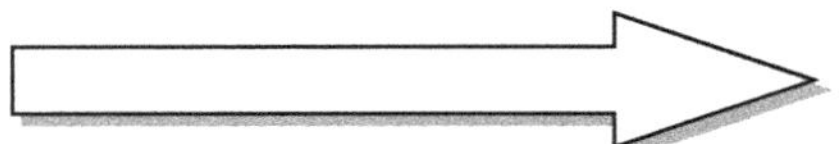

RECAPTURE

"For the Lord, the God of Israel says he hates divorce and cruel men. Therefore control your passions—let there be no divorcing of your wives [husbands]." Malachi 2:16 TLB, brackets added

God's chosen people had a false sense of security because of their privileged relationship with God. God in His mercy pleaded with His own people to return to a heart of reverence and obedience to Himself with the marital commitment being near the top of that list! The Book of Malachi contains only four chapters. Chapter two has only seventeen verses, and seven of those verses address the subject of divorce! God is not silent on this matter. God cares about divorce among His people! God meant what He said—and God said what He meant!

- **Read** Malachi 2:10-16 now.

Simply and strongly put, "God hates divorce!" There is nothing to misunderstand about how God feels about divorce. So, why are Christian couples finding themselves literally in divorce court? The answer is very simple, sin! There can be many different factors that cause Christian couples to end their marriages in divorce, but the root will always be traced back to sin in some manner, by either one or both partners.

Synonyms for "Divorce"

BREAK UP, DECOUPLE, DISASSOCIATE, DISCONNECT, DISJOIN, DISJOINT, DISSEVER, DISSOCIATE, DISUNITE, DIVIDE, SEPARATE, PART, RAMIFY, RESOLVE, SEVER, SPLIT, SUNDER, UNCOUPLE, UNLINK, UNYOKE

Let's begin to dissect this passage of Scripture from Malachi as it relates directly to the marriage commitment. **Please answer the following questions to the best of your ability:**

- Verse 10 is a *demand,* to remind us that we can actually profane the covenant of our fathers by dealing "treacherously" against a brother. For the sake of this study on marital commitment, who could your brother be from this verse?

- Verse 11 is an *indictment,* what has Judah done? Who could Judah represent?

- Verse 12 is a *warning,* what will happen to the one who has dealt treacherously and committed an abomination?

- Verse 13 is an *analysis,* what does God no longer regard or accept?

- Verse 14 is a *verdict,* what did God do for the divorced partner?

- Verse 15 is a *finding* of what went wrong. The finding proves the fundamental problem in the heart of the one who divorces their partner, what is it?

- Verse 16 is the *conclusion*. What does God say about divorce? What does God say about your spirit?

Word Study

You may have noticed all of the "legal" terms used in this section of the lesson to describe the nature of each verse in the passage of your study—that was intentional! Marriage is a legal contract! Christian men and women are bound by God and bound by the laws of their land to uphold their marital commitment.

In order to more fully appreciate the terms of this contract you will **look up** and **record dictionary definitions** for:

- Contract

- Promise

- Remain

- Fulfill

- Companion

- Witness

- Treacherous

- Wrong

- Hate

RECONNECT

Commitment

- Using your word study from the last section list three words that most closely describe your *attitude* of commitment towards your husband:

1. ____________________
2. ____________________
3. ____________________

- Would your husband be surprised by this or would he have used the same words to describe your attitude of commitment towards him?

- How does this make you feel?

- For further *insight* please **read 1 Corinthians 7:10** now. What does Paul say to wives about their husbands?

- Who does Paul say is giving this instruction?

- For further *instruction* by the Lord please **read Matthew 19:1-9** now.

When the Pharisees came to test Jesus they asked him about the subject of divorce. Loopholes towards God's original plan had already been well established amongst the Jews. The Pharisees thought this subject matter had become complicated and that extenuating circumstances could free a man from his marriage commitment. Jesus makes the matter uncomplicated by getting back to basics, the very Word of God!

"Do not move an ancient boundary stone set up by your forefathers."
Proverbs 22:28

- From verses 4 and 5 record the two most significant facts from Jesus' response to the Pharisees:

- From verse 6. Because a *husband and wife are no longer two but have become one,* what does Jesus say?

The Pharisees pursue the matter further being unsatisfied with Jesus' response. They proceed to point to Moses who had given a command that if married men wanted to divorce their wives that they *must give her a certificate of divorce.*

- From verse 8, why had Moses permitted them to divorce their wives?

- From verse 9, what does Jesus say about the one who divorces his wife?

- Jesus had finally shut the Pharisees up. Now look at who takes up the debate! From verse 10, who is speaking to Jesus now about the subject of divorce?

"The lamp of the LORD searches the spirit of a man; it searches out his inmost being."
Proverbs 20:27

The disciples had a difficult time receiving what Jesus said. In essence their response went like this, "If you can't get out of a bad marriage you are better off not marrying at all!" Jesus acknowledges their sarcastic remark as being closer to the truth than they probably thought. Verses eleven and twelve underscore the point that some people are simply not suited for marriage for a variety of reasons.

Self-Evaluation

- On a scale 1-5 (Five being the greatest), please rate yourself on your ability to commit in a general way. (Do you follow through on your commitments?)

  1 2 3 4 5

- Now make a short list of examples that illustrate your ability to commit in a general way. (In example: career, job, education, clubs, and ministry.)

- Now for your marital commitment. Are you presently one hundred percent committed to your husband in your marriage?

- Would your husband agree with your response about your own level of commitment to him?

- Do you recognize a pattern? How do you feel about this?

<u>The "opt-out card</u>"

Some men and women in marriage maintain an "opt-out card." They will remain in the marriage as long as they feel committed to it. But if the marriage becomes too difficult and they feel that there is no future, they will opt-out, they will divorce. ***Holding an "opt-out card" while married is simply <u>not</u> committing all one hundred percent of yourself to your marriage!***

This is where some Christian women get tricked; some Christian women actually forget that God knows their every thought! When a Christian woman is praying over a difficult marriage, and yet all the while is entertaining divorce as an option, she sets herself up for failure. How can God bless her prayers when she knowingly entertains divorce, something *God hates?*

In essence when a woman does this she is saying to God, "Lord help me in my marriage, but if You don't do what I 'm asking, I'll just have to divorce my husband. You leave me no other options."

"Victory had been within their grasp then and they had flung it away. What could a man do with these amateur soldiers who stopped fighting because they were tired?"

~ Elizabeth Goudge

A Novel

Often marriage counseling, including some Christian marriage counseling, will approach a difficult marriage with the idea of working on the specific complaints of the marriage hoping that if they can *fix* the complaints, the couple will re-commit to the marriage.

That is truly putting the cart before the horse. *Successful marriages begin and endure because of commitment!* The first thing couples need to do is to whole heartedly commit to their marriage and that will be their solid foundation on which to build and overcome the difficulties that can come with marriage!

Honor the Lord with your sincere commitment to your marriage so that you can put yourself in a position for God to bless your efforts!

- Have you ever or are you presently holding an "opt-out card?"

- If you answered yes, explain how you feel about this:

Loyalty

This portion of the lesson will deal specifically with fidelity in marriage. Marriage can survive many egregious failings, but infidelity is the one sin that will test a marriage like no other. Jesus said it could be the one thing that is a marriage breaker! Let's see what Scripture has to say about infidelity.

➢ Please **read** **Matthew 1:6** now.

✝ Complete this sentence directly from Matthew 1:6. *"Solomon was born to David by*

_________________________________."

What a sad epitaph for Bathsheba. She was not recorded in the lineage of Jesus by her name, but rather by what she did! She had been the wife of Uriah. Bathsheba and Uriah had *become one flesh through marriage*, and that's how the Holy Spirit remembers her.

Some would argue that the day King David saw her bathing on the roof and summoned her to him that she had no choice in the matter. There's always a choice! Whatever refusing David would have cost Bathsheba, if anything, it would have paled in comparison to what that sin cost both her and David, *"Then it happened on the seventh day that the child died."* 2 Samuel 12:18

➢ Please **read** **2 Samuel 12:1-25.**

- From verse 13, what did David say to Nathan? Note: It is important to acknowledge infidelity as sin, not only against the married partner, but also against the Lord.

- From verse 13, what did Nathan say to David?

- From verse 14, what did Nathan say happened as a result of this sin?

Unfortunately all of us know Christian couples that have committed this sin, and isn't it true the comments are summarized this way, "and I thought he/she was a Christian?"

Christians are held to a higher level of scrutiny and that's good! Yes it's true we are only saved sinners but as saved sinners we have free access to an all-powerful and all-knowing God. And whether the world truly understands this fact, they will ultimately still hold us accountable to it!

➢ **Read** and **record** **Hebrews 13:4** now.

✢ How should marriage be thought of?

✢ What does this verse say about the marriage bed (fidelity)?

✢ Who will God judge?

Make It Personal

How confident does your husband feel concerning your fidelity? Circle the number on this scale of 1-5 (Five being the greatest).

1 2 3 4 5

- Would your husband rate your fidelity the same way?

- How does this make you feel?

- Fidelity also is a matter of the heart, **read Matthew 5:27-30 now.** Please **record** Matthew **5:28.**

"When we find ourselves looking to the future because we aren't content with today, may God give us a peace of mind that lets us rest where He has placed us."

~ Emile Barnes
Whispers of Prayer

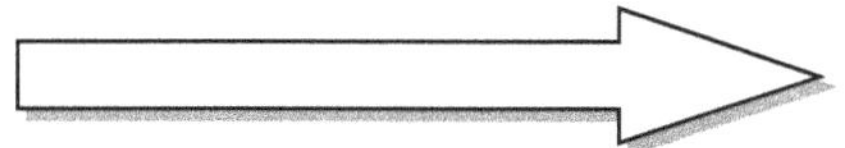

REDIRECT

Faithfulness in marriage encompasses: mind, heart, and body. When one or both partners become unfaithful, in any of these areas, they have broken their vows. Repentance before God is necessary, and words and acts of contrition are most helpful.

If you are someone who has broken your wedding vows whether in mind, heart or body, do the right thing! Confess your sin to God so that you can be made clean. And if you feel that you would benefit by sharing this with a trusted godly friend or counselor, do so as soon as possible

Infidelity doesn't have to be a marriage breaker! There is always hope with a God named Redeemer! Your Redeemer is able to redeem broken vows, broken trust, and even a broken heart. If you have fallen in this area of your marriage and are truly repentant and have taken steps of contrition, let go of your old sin, God has! You are clean and new! *"Woman, where are they? ...neither do I condemn you; go your way. From now on sin no more."* John 8:10,11 NASB

If you are a married woman who has experienced infidelity by your husband in mind, heart, or body, you have experienced betrayal. Your heart will have a very difficult time learning to trust again. Bitterness will also be knocking at your door. Don't let bitterness in. Once bitterness sets its roots in your soul you will only be further robbed!

"The things which are impossible with men are possible with God."
Luke 18:27

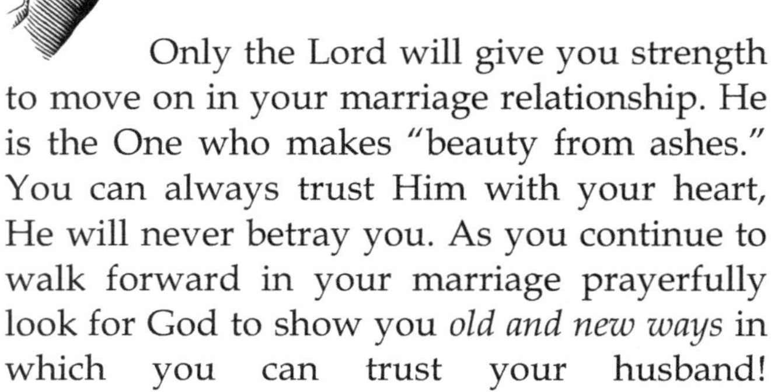

Only the Lord will give you strength to move on in your marriage relationship. He is the One who makes "beauty from ashes." You can always trust Him with your heart, He will never betray you. As you continue to walk forward in your marriage prayerfully look for God to show you *old and new ways* in which you can trust your husband!

DAILY HOMEWORK

You may have taken traditional wedding vows the day you were married and you may not have. Either way, most people know what traditional wedding vows are. The Daily Homework for this lesson will ask that you ***recommit in mind, heart, and body*** to your husband.

For each of the next seven days please take the time to pray over the designated vow for that day. For an added blessing share with your husband the vow for that day and let him know that you have recommitted yourself to him in that way! **Record the date as you complete each vow.**

Day one) "To have and to hold from this day forward."

Day two) "To honor and to obey."

Day three) "For better or for worse."

Day four) "For richer or for poorer."

Day five) "In sickness and in health."

Day six) "To love and to cherish."

Day seven) "From this day forward until death do us part."

If you had difficulty with any of these marriage vows, would you please take time now and write what you are feeling as a prayer to the Lord asking Him to help you integrate these vows into your mind, heart, and body. The Lord wants to help you with this. Be faithful to do what you can with a sincere heart—and look for the Lord to bless your faithfulness!

DIARY

- ✓ Have you gained any new perspective(s) about your marriage commitment to your husband as a result of doing this lesson? If so please explain.

- ✓ What does it mean to you to be a faithful wife; mind, heart, and body?

- ✓ How has God personally ministered to you through this study?

Notes

Lesson Seven

Forgetting What Lies Behind

Disappointments, regrets, pain, wounds, and even suffering often are a fact of life. Sometimes these facts enter the marriage and can become stumbling stones, walls, and deep valleys that cause couples to struggle throughout their marriage. Moving forward with any momentum at all is almost impossible if one or both married partners are continuously looking back at painful memories.

The Lord knows how difficult it is for anyone who has been deeply wounded, or who has deeply wounded, to move forward—and so He gave us plenty of Scripture on this very subject matter to set us straight, to encourage us, and to show us the way out of the pit of painful memories!

This lesson will focus on letting go of what holds you. You will dig deeply into Scripture looking for hope and for practical ways that can help anyone who lives in the past to move forward into the future of the great plans that God has for His beloved!

Let's begin to *recapture* truth from Scripture on this very subject.

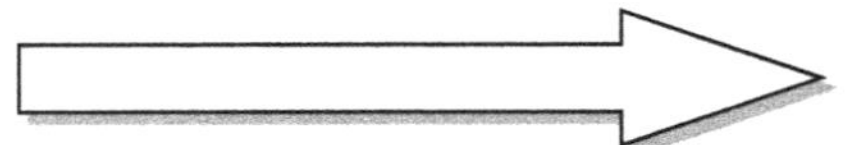

RECAPTURE

"...but one thing I do: forgetting what lies behind and reaching forward to what lies ahead...."
Philippians 3:13

From this portion of Scripture Paul wrote about his past life before being found in Christ Jesus. Whether it was praiseworthy or worthy of profound shame, it was all the same to Paul. How could that be? How was Paul able to put all things, good and bad, behind him as the same? Paul made it simple! Instead of trying to do many things—he said he did just one thing! Paul couldn't change the past, but Paul could *actively reach forward to what lies ahead!*

➢ **Read Philippians 3:1-16 now**.

Paul sets the stage by proclaiming that the believer is of *the true circumcision,* and that the believer *does not put confidence in the flesh.* Paul proceeds to list his many credentials in the *flesh* and yet he concludes that these credentials are *but rubbish*! This is the point: the flesh is weak and will fail you! That's why so many Christians do have regrets, disappointments, and painful memories!

- According to verse 9, where does our righteousness come from, and on what basis?

- From verse 10, what does Paul say about suffering?

- In your own words, explain what you think it means to have *fellowship in Christ's sufferings*?

- In verse 12 Paul expresses himself in this way, "...**but I press on** in order that I may lay hold of that for which also I was laid hold of by Christ Jesus." What do you think Paul means by this statement?

- Can you identify with this type of attitude?

- How important could this attitude be in the process of moving forward and not looking back?

- In verse 13 Paul repeats his point, he has *not obtained it* nor *has he laid hold of it **yet**!* What is the **"it"** that Paul is speaking about? (Take your time with this, the answer can be subtle).

- In verse 14 Paul reiterates the fact that he will *press on*. What is Paul pressing toward?

- Now that's perspective! Many people, including Christians, fear the future because of the past. They fear the unknown as if there were no God and no plan. Please **<u>read</u> and <u>record</u> Psalm 139:16 now.**

- When did God first see you?

Warren Weirsbe has made a thought provoking point from his commentary on Philippians, he says this: "…we are accustomed to saying 'past, present, future,' but we should view time as flowing from the future into the present and then into the past."

- What has been written in God's book?

- What type of *days* will you have?

- See if you can pull together the facts you learned from Psalm 139:16 and the exhortation you studied in Philippians 3:1-16 into one statement in your own words: (Keep this simple. You may want to review Warren Wiersbe's perspective as well).

Word Study

Record dictionary definitions for:

- Behind

- Obtain

- Reach

- Goal

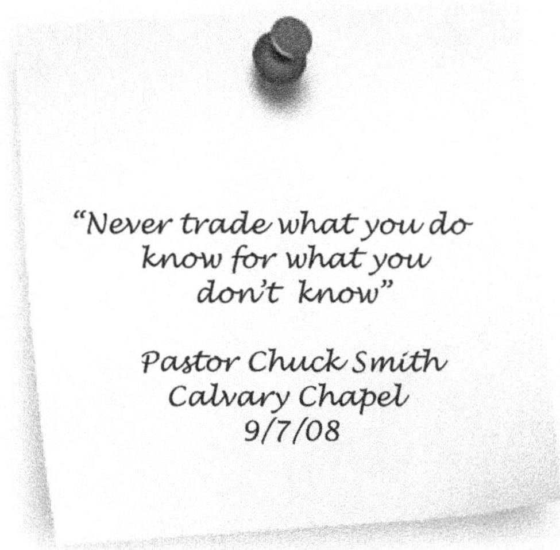

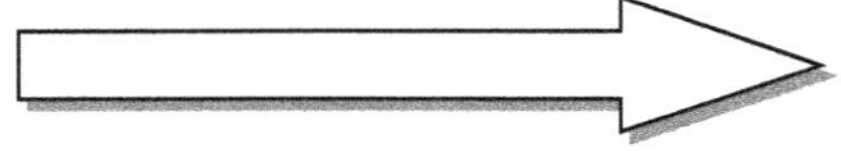

RECONNECT

Moving Forward

- Review your word study from the last section. Which word(s) from your **word study**, if applied, could benefit your current perspective about the past?

  Explain:

- This is your next question: **Is it more important for you to remember the past, or to look forward to the future?**

To see how well you really line up with your last answer, circle the answer that best fits:

- I think about what has been…

Never Sometimes Always

- I think about my future with hope…

Never Sometimes Always

- Whatever you spend your time thinking about reveals where you are in relation to the exhortation Paul gives in Philippians 3:13. How do you feel about your current status?

It can be very difficult to let go of the past. But when we don't, we are at risk of turning past memories into an idol! When our past memories become bigger than the God who holds our future, we have turned the past into an idol!

"There is surely a future hope for you, and your hope will not be cut off."
Proverbs 23:18

- If you are someone who dwells on the past, how could Paul's statement, *"but one thing I do,"* help you move forward and let go of the past?

A Type of Idolatry

When Christians worry, hold onto pain, and become angry over the past they are at risk of turning memories and emotions into an idol. When memories and emotions about what has been consume your every thought, you are no longer putting God first. You have put your past on the Throne, instead of God!

There is an interesting insight found in Psalm 106:36, *"And they served their idols, which became a snare to them."* The Hebrew word ('atsab, aw-tsawb') used for idol in this verse means: a literal *idol or image*. The root word ('atsab, aw-tsab') means: *to worry, pain, or anger*.

- Notice Psalm 106:36 says that *"they served their idols…"* How might a Christian serve the *idol* of worry, pain, or anger?

- Have you ever *served the idol* of worry, painful memories, or anger?

- How could this become a *snare* to the Christian? (You may want to consult the dictionary definition of the word *snare* for added insight)

- **Read** and **record** **Exodus 20:3 now.**

- What does **1 Corinthians 10:14** say?

Obviously there is a difference between actual idol worship—where a person believes in a deity embodied in some type of object, versus the Christian who holds onto the past in a negative way. But the point remains: ***anything*** that takes precedence above the God of the Bible is an idol!

- It could be very helpful to make a list now of what lies in the past that you need to let go of. Would you **honestly** and **prayerfully** record your thoughts now, and lay them at the finished work of the cross of Christ? (You may want to record the date as a memorial.)

"Hatred stirs up dissension, but love covers over all wrongs."
Proverbs 10:12

The Nature of Forgiveness

- Please read **Ephesians 4:30-32 now**.

- **Record** Ephesians 4:31.

- From Ephesians 4:31, how should the Christian deal with these negative characteristics?

- What do you think this means in a practical way?

Christians know that they are to forgive offenses. But sometimes Christians only <u>think</u> about forgiving the offender, instead of actually <u>forgiving</u> the offender! Think about how many times you have actually forgiven an offense – it might not be as often as you may think!

- From verse 32, how are you to forgive?

Are you someone who feels like you need to tell people when they have hurt your feelings, even if you suspect that it was done unintentionally? Some Christians confuse this approach with the scriptural instruction given by Jesus in Matthew 18:15-17. This instruction is a guideline for discipline within the church body and should not necessarily be applied to the person who has caused hurt feelings unintentionally.

- Please **<u>read</u> Matthew 18:15-17 now**.

- What has the *brother* done?

- What should the Christian do for his *brother*?

- **Now read Matthew 18:21-22.**

- How often are you to forgive your brother?

Forgiveness and Apologies

- What is the *Golden Rule*? **Read and record Matthew 7:12.**

- Do you think you have ever hurt or injured anyone else?

- Would you want their forgiveness? Explain why:

Many years ago a movie titled "Love Story" made a romantic statement popular, "Love means never having to say you're sorry." The truth is that the more you truly love—the more likely you'll want to say you are sorry when you should!

This is one of the most difficult things for people in general to do, including Christians! How many times have you, or has someone said to you, "I'm sorry, but I ...?" When a person says that they are sorry and then proceeds to explain why they did or said what they did instead of just leaving it as an apology—they take away the true sentiment and <u>power</u> of the apology. They also have not taken full ownership of what they have done.

Apologies with excuses or defenses aren't true confessions of wrong doings. Those types of apologies don't really accomplish their intended purpose!

- Now **read Colossians 3:12-13.**

- As those who have been *chosen of God, holy and beloved,* what are you to put on?

- Why?

- Are you someone who has a difficult time saying, "I'm sorry"? Circle the appropriate answer.

Yes No Sometimes

- Explain your answer:

- When was the last time you genuinely said, "I'm sorry," without an excuse?

Healing Can Come

> **Read and record James 5:16 now.**

- What two things are Christians to do for each other from the instructions found in James 5:16?

- What can be the result of doing these two things?

- Are you someone who needs healing? If you are, will you be willing to do what James said can bring about healing?

"If you have raced with men on foot and they have worn you out, how can you compete with horses? If you stumble in a safe country, how will you manage in the thickets of the Jordan?"

God's response to Jeremiah's complaint.

Jeremiah 12:5

- What is the concluding statement made by James in this verse?

You have just completed a biblical step by step study on how to let go of what holds you. You have been led through the *perspective* of letting go through your study in Philippians chapter three. You have studied the dangers of *idolatry* as it relates to holding on to the past through consuming thoughts. You have studied the *nature of forgiveness* and the importance of an *apology*. Finally, you have discovered how true *healing* can be accomplished from a biblical perspective through James simple instructions!

All of these points can be a powerful resource for anyone who lives in the pit of the past! The choice is yours—you can choose to let go and move forward, or you can continue to remain where you are and allow what has been to rob you of what can be!

- Prayer is an essential for the Christian. It is through prayer that we get linked up with God and gain His perspective about our future, present life, and the past. Please briefly describe your prayer life:

- Could your prayer life benefit from more diligence and structure? If so, what do you intend to do about that?

REDIRECT

Struggling with disappointments, regrets, pain, and wounds will put a strain on any marriage. Whether those struggles originate from outside the marriage or are found in the marriage, they must be overcome! It is important to say at this time that God does not expect a woman to stay in a continuously abusive marriage. **If you need help ascertaining what "continuous abuse" may be, please consult with a trusted pastor or another woman who is very mature in the Lord.**

Forgetting what lies behind can be difficult to do, but not impossible! The term "to forget" in the Bible means *"no longer to be influenced by or affected by."* You cannot actually forget the past, but you can choose to not let the past have a controlling influence on your life. There are some things that are good to remember, to protect you and to keep you from making similar mistakes. However, to allow a painful past to control your future is to let yourself be robbed of what God has planned for you!

To quote Warren Wiersbe again from his commentary on Philippians chapter three,

"Forgetting those things which are behind does not suggest an impossible feat of mental and psychological gymnastics…it simply means that we break the power of the past by living for the future. We cannot change the past, but we can change the meaning of the past."

Struggling with what *lies behind* doesn't always include painful memories or old wounds. Maybe you are a woman who needs to *forget what lies behind* in this way: a successful career, financial income, education, health, your home, friends, ministry, or even your church fellowship.

Sometimes married women need to let go of good things, even hopes and dreams. What do you do? These are matters truly intended for prayer. Only the Lord knows the plans He has for you. You must seek and gain His heart and His mind about these matters. If the Lord is asking you to let go of the past in anyway, or even to let go of something you have hoped for in the future, remember, He has your very best in mind! By letting go and *forgetting what lies behind,* or ahead, you will be wholeheartedly trusting in the Lord! This can actually turn how you view what has been, and what is to be, around for yourself. You may even find yourself actually embracing the life the Lord has chosen for you, for the very first time!

"For He has done all things well" *Mark 7:37*

Sometimes it isn't what has been done to us that *holds* us. Sometimes it is what *we* have done in the past that *holds* us. Paul understood this better than probably any of the other apostles of Jesus Christ. Paul said this of himself, *"For you have heard of my former manner of life in Judaism, how I used to persecute the church of God beyond measure, and tried to destroy it..."* Galatians 1:13

> "God will never ask you to do anything for Him that He expects you to do without Him."
>
> ~ Roy Lessin
>
> *A Fruitful Life*

Maybe you can relate to the extreme measures that Paul went to in an attempt to accomplish his purpose. Maybe you can relate to the realization that you have even tried to destroy something that you now realize was very wrong to do. Maybe you have been hateful. Maybe you have been hurtful. Maybe you have been foolish. Maybe you have even been blind!

Paul is our example. Paul received forgiveness of his sins, and pressed forward to the prize of the upward call of God in Christ Jesus! Paul would not allow what he had done to keep him from his call by God for ministry, or to even keep himself from enjoying the fellowship of those he had once persecuted!

If you need to let go of what you have done in the past, will you take time now and prayerfully lay those things down, and press forward? It may be helpful to share this with a trusted friend who is mature in Christ.

DAILY HOMEWORK

The secret to Paul's success over his destructive past was to do *one thing*! In the Daily Homework section you will prayerfully and consciously **make note of how you are pursuing *the goal of the upward call of God in Christ Jesus.*** This is most critical in *redirecting* your thoughts and attitudes.

You are being asked to **start each day in prayer**. Sincerely ask the Lord to show you how to pursue this goal. If you take time with this and sincerely wait for the Lord to speak very simply to you—you will be off to a good start in gaining the same perspective and attitude that was in Paul! Do this **diligently** for one week and see what happens!

Day one) Record the date and your thoughts from your prayer time.

Day two) Record the date and your thoughts from your prayer time.

Day three) Record the date and your thoughts from your prayer time.

Day four) Record the date and your thoughts from your prayer time.

Day five) Record the date and your thoughts from your prayer time.

Day six) Record the date and your thoughts from your prayer time.

Day seven) Record the date and your thoughts from your prayer time.

DIARY

- ✓ Evaluate and record your *thoughts* about your own personal past in light of doing this study.

- ✓ Did you discover a new appreciation for the importance of letting go of the past? Share your thoughts.

- ✓ Was there a Scripture verse or passage that particularly ministered to you through this study? If so explain.

Notes

Lesson Eight

What Have You Gained?

You may recall the theme verse for this series of lessons, *"...for from the first day that you set your heart on understanding this and on humbling yourself before your God, your words were heard..."* Daniel 1-:12. The Hebrew phrase to *set your heart* means to "gain understanding."

You have studied seven specific key areas of marriage. Now you will review each lesson and find a place to make notes on how you have gained understanding about your marriage, your husband, and the unique role that God has designed for wives.

<u>Lesson One *"Reality!"*</u>

"Finally, brothers, whatever is true, whatever is noble, whatever is right, whatever is pure, whatever is lovely, whatever is admirable – if anything is excellent or praiseworthy – think about such things." Philippians 4:8

What have you gained?

- Favorite Scripture verse from this lesson:

- Favorite section from this lesson (please explain why):

Lesson Two *"Blessings"*

"I will bless those who bless you, and whoever curses you I will curse; and all the peoples on earth will be blessed through you." Genesis 12:3

What have you gained?

- Favorite Scripture verse from this lesson:

- Favorite section from this lesson (please explain why):

Lesson Three *"Your Body Is Not Your Own"*

"The wife's body does not belong to her alone but also to her husband. In the same way, the husband's body does not belong to him alone but also to his wife." 1Corinthians 7:4

What have you gained?

- Favorite Scripture verse from this lesson:

- Favorite section from this lesson (please explain why):

<u>Lesson Four *"The Submissive Wife, Get Real!"*</u>

"For this is the way the holy women of the past who put their hope in God used to make themselves beautiful. They were submissive to their own husbands." 1 Peter 3:5

What have you gained?

- Favorite Scripture verse from this lesson:

- Favorite section from this lesson (please explain why):

<u>Lesson Five *"Raise The Bar And Don't Cross Those Lines!"*</u>

"...the Lord forbid that I should do such a thing to my master, the Lord's anointed, or lift my hand against him; for he is the anointed of the Lord." 1 Samuel 24:5

What have you gained?

- Favorite Scripture verse from this lesson:

- Favorite section from this lesson (please explain why):

<u>Lesson Six *"Commitment and Loyalty"*</u>

"For the Lord, the God of Israel, says he hates divorce and cruel men. Therefore control your passions – let there be no divorcing of your wives [husbands]." Malachi 2:16 TLB, brackets added

What have you gained?

- Favorite Scripture verse from this lesson:

- Favorite section from this lesson (please explain why):

<u>Lesson Seven *"Forgetting What Lies Behind"*</u>

"…but one thing I do: forgetting what lies behind and reaching forward to what lies ahead…" Philippians 3:13

What have you gained?

- Favorite Scripture verse from this lesson:

- Favorite section from this lesson (please explain why):

Reviews and Testimonies

"There is no doubt that the institution of marriage is under attack. This study, ***BOOT CAMP for the Married Woman's Soul,*** is the best one that I have ever done on this subject. It cuts to the heart of the matter and addresses the root causes of conflict and trouble in marriage. I heartily recommend it! If you would like insight into your marriage and would like to strengthen and enhance your relationship with your husband, this study will help you reach those goals."
Georgia Riojas
Women's Ministry Leader, Worship Leader

"...We live in a time when marriage is held with so little regard that over half of all marriages end in divorce. And this fact is equally true in Christian marriages. This should not be so! Would you begin by asking the Lord to give you a greater perspective of His view of marriage; and would you make a personal commitment to love the institution of marriage as He does and to hate divorce as He does? ***BOOT CAMP for the Married Woman's Soul*** will help you do just that!"
Diane Jackson
Harvest Christian Fellowship
Editor, Mentoring Matters Coordinator

"I am so thankful God led me to ***BOOT CAMP for the Married Woman's Soul.*** I hadn't realized how out of shape my heart was! I've done other marriage Bible studies and this is the first one to really dig deep into a woman's heart. God spoke to me through this study about reigning in my thought life; obeying the Lord in every situation and trusting Him to work things out according to His plan. I recommend this study for every married woman!"
Ginger Fero, RN
Women's Ministry Leader

More about Christi . . .

Christi began women's ministry nearly forty years ago in her home church, Harvest Christian Fellowship in Riverside, California. She serves as a Bible study teacher and coordinator assisting with training women in spiritual leadership roles.

Christi and her husband, Larry, have been married for 45 years and live in Southern California. Christi is a homemaker and considers that her primary ministry.

Visit Christi's website at: www.christirobillard.com

All of Christi's books are available on amazon

www.ingramcontent.com/pod-product-compliance
Lightning Source LLC
Chambersburg PA
CBHW081139090426
42736CB00018B/3404

* 9 7 8 0 6 1 5 7 1 0 7 8 5 *